SCHOLASTIC

D0246286

YOU CAN

Improve
your children's
WRITING

Celia Warren

**FOR AGES
4-7**

"...pupils continue to find
it difficult to produce their
best writing unaided.."
DfES

Acknowledgements

Author
Celia Warren

Editor
Sally Gray

Development Editor
Kate Pedlar

Series Designer
Joy Monkhouse

Cover Designer
Anna Oliwa

Cover illustration
© Punchstock/ImageSource

Design and Illustrations
Q2a Media

Text © Celia Warren
© 2007 Scholastic Ltd

Designed using Adobe InDesign

Published by Scholastic Ltd
Villiers House
Clarendon Avenue
Leamington Spa
Warwickshire CV32 5PR

www.scholastic.co.uk

Printed by Bell and Bain Ltd.
1 2 3 4 5 6 7 8 9 7 8 9 0 1 2 3 4 5 6

British Library Cataloguing-in-Publication Data
A catalogue record for this book is available from the British Library.
ISBN 0-439-945-305
ISBN 978-0439-94530-1

The right of Celia Warren to be identified as the author of this work has been asserted by her in accordance with the Copyright, Designs and Patents Act 1988.

Every effort has been made to trace copyright holders for the works reproduced in this book, and the publishers apologise for any inadvertent omissions.

Contents

Contents

Introduction

This book aims to help you inspire children to develop basic writing skills and achieve their highest capabilites. As infant teachers, you carry the great responsibility and privilege of instilling good habits in children – from how they hold a pencil to how they construct a sentence. This book offers tips and activites to help children increase their confidence and develop their skills in poetry, story- and non-fiction writing. It also seeks to increase your satisfaction as you observe the children's interest and enjoyment in creative and purposeful writing.

Preparing to write

Are there pencils enough and to spare? Are they sharpened? Are whiteboards and scrap paper handy for draft work? Can children help themselves to materials with minimum disruption? A practical, writer-friendly environment will influence children's attitude to writing. For example, it is important that they know where to look for help with frequent spellings and punctuation. Lists of common words are a great help. An alphabet on display is another handy resource.

Celebrating the written word

When their writing is displayed, children will take a pride in their own and their friends' efforts. If possible, keep these at children's eye-level for them to read and re-read. Mounting and labelling their work neatly demonstrates that you value their efforts. If wall-space is limited, there are other ways to celebrate your children's efforts and, most importantly, enable their words to be read. Big book format class anthologies preserve and celebrate work while remaining accessible to the young writers themselves. Concertina books in the library corner and in corridor space, on top of book shelves, provide eye-level display. Children's 'by-lines' given due prominence are important validation. This reminds children that they are authors just as much as the writers of published books.

After the how – the why!

In infant classrooms, the teaching of the mechanics of writing inevitably prevails. The National Literacy Framework provides a wonderful basis for systematic teaching of word-, sentence- and text-level skills; the writer's tools of trade. Make sure you remind children of the purpose of gaining these skills. Even early writers can experience the delights of creating stories and poems, of expressing opinions, sharing news, sending letters and cards, writing captions and annotations. A major aim of this book is to act in advocacy for the whole rationale of the writing experience. It explores and encourages outlets for children to discover the joys of writing.

You Can... # Create a writing-friendly classroom

As children approach their first day at school, friends and relations will explain that they 'will learn to read and write'. The two go hand in hand and there is no reason why children should not do both on their very first day in school. It would be a shame to disappoint them!

Thinking points

● One in ten children is left-handed. Make sure that you can form all letters with both hands. You will need to be ambidextrous to guide the children's writing hands.

● Practise air-writing letters backwards. In front of a class, demonstrate each letter-formation in the air. Your letters need to be back to front so that they are the right way round for the children to watch and copy.

● Encourage parents, if teaching their children to write their names before they start school, to use lower-case letters (onset capitals apart) in preference to all capitals, to avoid confusion when they use lower-case letters at school.

Tips, ideas and activities

● Arrange children's seating so that all have ample space. Seat left-handed children to the left of right-handed children to allow elbow room for all.

● For air-writing and letter-recognition activities, have the children on a carpeted area, where they can concentrate on watching you.

● If the children are working on loose paper, make sure they have something firm, but giving, to rest on. Hard table-tops are not conducive to comfortable handwriting.

● Prepare a supply of wide-lined paper, already marked with a dot, top left, to remind children where to start writing. (This is especially important if they are using pre-punched A4 paper that you will file.)

● Write the day and date on the board before children come into the classroom. Encourage them to read this first thing each day. After their name, the date will be the second most regular thing they write.

● Tape each child's name on the table in front of them for easy reference. Explain that they will write their name most days.

● Make a set of flash cards of children's names. On their first day, ask them to put up their hand when they see their name. Hand them their card. They have read on their first day!

● Prepare sheets of A4 paper with a large rectangle centred inside a narrow margin. Ask the children to decorate the outside margin with coloured crayons. Meanwhile, help each child to write their first name in the centre rectangle. Some may be doing this for the first time. Guide their hand over a lightly pencilled line if necessary. Correct any poor pencil-holding techniques. They have written on their first day!

You Can... **Help children to develop pencil control**

The number of physical contortions people adopt when wielding a pen never ceases to amaze! If only they had been taught patiently and consistently as infants how to hold a pencil, how much more comfortable they would be, and how much more enjoyable the process of writing would be. They might not even need to stick their tongue out in the process!

Thinking points

● Children may forget their dinner money, their notes, their PE kit, but never their hands, so pencil-control activities can always be practised.

● Make sure that children's hands are clean before they begin writing. A sticky pencil and a soiled page are not the best starting points for good handwriting.

● As far as pencil control is concerned, consistency, perseverance and patience in the early days pay huge dividends later: stick with it! Other activities that develop the muscles and dexterity required for good pencil grip need to be provided regularly – for example, manipulating malleable materials such as play dough.

● Find out whether your school can supply plastic slide-on pencil grips for children with less advanced motor control. The triangular cross-section encourages good grip and hand position and can be very useful in the early stages of writing.

Tips, ideas and activities

● Before children can begin to write they must have pencil control. This will only come easily if they are holding their pencil correctly and comfortably. Anything new is awkward at first, but it is worth insisting that the children persevere. Remind pencil 'fist-clutchers' that they are not swatting flies or batting a ball.

● Children who tense up to write may keep breaking their pencil lead as they press too hard. Humour helps children to relax – tell them that you want them to tickle the page. When they get it right, make the ticklish paper giggle.

● Before encouraging the children to attempt fine pencil control, let them get used to holding the pencil and keeping the point in contact with the page. Demonstrate on a whiteboard how to draw a line without lifting the pen from the page. Make your line travel slowly all over the page, crossing lines already formed, looping and zigzagging. Tell the children that your pen has had a lovely time! Now ask them to 'take their pencil for a walk' – all over the page. Allow the children to colour in the spaces, trying to keep inside the lines where possible.

● Prepare sets of wiggly and zigzagging tramlines across the page for children to trace over. Include a start-dot to the left of each pattern. This not only develops pencil control, but also teaches left-to-right orientation. Remind the children to keep their pencil point in contact with the page, not lifting it until it reaches the end.

● Reinforce pencil contact, and left-to-right progress, by drawing an animal on the left-hand side and its home on the right. Their pencil leads the animal home. (If they lift their pencil it will make the creature jump and it may get lost!)

You Can... Use a multi-sensory approach to writing

Children have heightened senses, but these may develop at different paces and will take different levels of prominence as each child matures. Wherever practicable, involve as many senses as possible in the writing process. For example, you may create a calm and soothing atmosphere, conducive to a relaxed approach to handwriting, by playing some gentle classical music.

Thinking points

● There is a natural rhythm to writing that only comes with practice. Young children learning to write are having to combine motor skills, pattern recognition and memory skills, visual, spatial and directional skills – this can prove a very steep learning curve for some.

● Display an alphabet chart around the walls – low enough for children to see, but high enough for them to see over others' heads when seated at their tables.

● Create a 'sounds' table displaying objects beginning with a letter that the children are practising that week. Invite the children to bring in items to add to the table. Include a small blackboard or whiteboard (and wiper) on the table for the children to practise the letter at intervals during each day.

Tips, ideas and activities

● Offer multi-sensory options for children just beginning to form letters. Writing and rewriting in a sand tray is fun, tactile and immediate. Mistakes can be shaken off, literally. (New unused cat litter trays make good table-top sand trays for writing.)

● Create sets of feely letter-shapes in diverse materials such as felt and fine sandpaper to provide finger-tracing practice prior to pencilling letters. Exploit the directional stroke of fake fur fabric to indicate starting direction.

● Use finger paints for children to 'feel' the shape of letters as they form them.

● As a parallel activity to pencil work, let children form letters from modelling clay. Ask the children to form the letters of a word that is a reading blind-spot. By forming each letter in Plasticine, while repeating the word, the children will be helped to remember and recognise it. In this way, early 'writing skills' complement early reading skills.

● Play a game of 'copycats', pairing children of mixed ability. Starting with the more able writer, one child writes any letter; the other must copy it. The game continues, but no letter must be repeated, until a time limit is called.

● Overcome fear of failure by using easily wiped individual whiteboards. Mistakes can be quickly corrected.

● Reinforce progress and confidence by inviting children to demonstrate their new-found skills. Invite children to come out and write a prescribed letter on the board. Save the trickier letters, or letter strings, for more able writers and the simpler letters, such as *i* and *o*, for the less confident.

● Use dots and arrows to remind children in which direction to begin their letter. Regularly check that no bad habits are creeping in. A little formal practice of lines of letters 'on parade' will give you the chance to get around the whole class.

You Can... Ease children into writing

When learning to play an instrument, we have to learn the technique for producing a note – any sound will do. We then have to learn fingering for specific notes and understand musical notation. But what is our motivation? What do we really want? We want to play a recognisable tune, to make music. The same goes for writing. Don't let children lose sight of the purpose behind their efforts. It will encourage them to know what doors are opening up to them.

Thinking points

● When introducing books, make sure that you point out the author's name. Explain that the words in the book were written by a real person. The children may not realise this.

● Even before they have written a story, children are already authors. When they play 'mums and dads' in the playground they are making up a story. Aesop never wrote a word – but consider how many more people enjoy his work thanks to the fact that his stories were eventually written down.

● Making opportunities for children to retell stories orally in their own words will prepare them well for when they begin to write stories. Prompt them with sequential words and phrases, such as *first*, *next*, and at *last*.

Tips, ideas and activities

● Introduce the concept of writing for a purpose. Children will soon understand the purpose of writing their own name (to distinguish their belongings; to help retrieve their work from a pile; to state authorship and to give credit to their work displayed on the wall).

● Involve the children in labelling – their table's pot of crayons or pencils, boxes for constructive play, scissors, paints, drawers of paper. It won't hurt if areas are labelled twice, by you and the children. Take every opportunity to link reading and writing in the children's minds. Once the connection is made, the incentive is there to write.

● Writing single words is an easily achievable target for early writing. Pull out your shopping list. Let the children see how you wrote it. Discuss why you wrote it. Together, write a shopping list for a hamster or a to-do list for Cinderella.

● Write a lost-property list of things found around the school. This could be real or made up.

● Present children with an alphabet written vertically. Ask them to create an alphabetical list. Give them a theme such as foods, animals or toys.

● Show how word order matters when writing. Ask the children to write a word that describes them in positive terms followed by their own name: *Sensible Adam*; *Kind Sunita*; *Funny Sam*.
  ● Extend these descriptive names into simple sentences by adding a verb using the present participle: *Sensible Adam is cooking*; *Kind Sunita is helping*; *Funny Sam is joking*.
  ● In your plenary, create one of yourself to show how pleased you are with them: *Tall Miss Brown is smiling*.

● Encourage the children to use single words or short phrases to add captions to wall-displays.

● Introduce speech bubbles into the children's drawings. Encourage them to make their characters speak!

You Can... **Provide supportive writing aids**

Levels of success in early learning are greatly influenced by a combination of teacher expectation and child confidence – one feeding the other. You cannot be everywhere at once, reinforcing your class teaching at an individual level by providing prompts. A well organised and resourced classroom helps children to develop independence (which also raises self-esteem) and enables them to help themselves.

Thinking points

● Remember that praise for effort and achievement breeds further effort and increased success. Make sure that you always make time to encourage children's attempts at writing and celebrate their successes during group and circle times.

● Many children enjoy being given their own areas of responsibility – so appoint pencil and paper monitors to sharpen pencils, distribute paper, and so on, to avoid all children being on the move at once.

● Consider inviting parents in to help individuals who are struggling to keep their mind on the task at hand. An adult hand pointing and encouraging can be very effective at keeping a child on target.

● Remember that young children find it hard to sit still for long periods of time and short bursts are better than long drawn-out sessions!

Tips, ideas and activities

● Make sure that all children know where resources are kept and instigate a 'put it back where you found it' habit.

● Decide on a policy for correcting mistakes. (Check first whether there is a whole-school policy). Are erasers permitted and, if so, must the children ask first for adult assistance? Erasers can become a bad habit that is hard to break. Writing an X after a mistake – or bracketing the error – and starting the word again can work just as well.

● Children who have difficulty with left-right orientation will find it harder to master writing skills. As a cue, display a sheet of paper, correctly oriented, margin and any file-perforations to the left, the prompt words *Name* and *Date* on the top line, and a starting dot two lines below (leaving a space) labelled *Title* and, two lines lower, a starting dot with the words *Start here* or *Write*. This at-a-glance prompt encourages independence and allows the children to check their work.

● Some children can copy from a board quite easily. Others will require a copy in front of them in order to keep up.

● Children finding information from books, or a spelling dictionary spelling can find it tricky to transfer from one to the other. Supply arrow-shaped sticky notes to help them keep their place – pointed at the word or sentence.

● Provide individual spelling books and frequent-word lists so that children have their own reference close at hand.

● Displays of useful words linked to writing activities are a great asset: question words; story beginnings; joining words, and so on. Don't allow walls to become too busy, rather, change the display to suit the activity. Laminate lists that you use regularly so that they can be stored and changed over quickly without damage. Vary the colour of ink and card for ease of reference.

You Can... Prompt children to take pride in their writing

'Look what I can do!' Every child wants to demonstrate a new-found skill or achievement. They want their efforts to be recognised and their ability admired. Approval and positive reinforcement is essential if children are to build on their success. Verbal praise and 'showing the whole class' are good starting points, but more permanent and formal expressions are helpful, too.

Thinking points

● If children know that you value their finished work, they will probably take more pride in its production. Make sure that you have a plan for their finished writing and inspire them by telling them in advance what this plan is.

● If children will be reading their writing aloud, remind them that careful lettering, spacing and punctuation will make this later task easier.

● Remind children always to put their name on their writing. This will encourage a sense of ownership, promoting the concept that what they write is a part of themselves.

● Are the materials you provide clean, fresh and inviting? Creased paper and blunt pencils can be very disheartening. Crisp paper and sharp pencils on the other hand, are encouraging.

Tips, ideas and activities

● If children are to underline a heading, make sure that rulers are available and that they use them. Demonstrate how to keep a ruler still while drawing a line. Encourage younger children to help each other in this process, steadying each other's ruler as they draw along its edge.

● Make sure that you provide regular handwriting practice where content is provided, so that children can concentrate on the writing only, developing an even, consistent script.

● Teach children how to use omission/insertion marks so that words left out can be written elsewhere on the page rather than squashed in illegibly.

● Show that you value the children's work by the manner in which you treat it. Collect and store loose sheets of writing carefully to avoid them becoming bent, creased or trodden on through a paper avalanche!

● Mount work creatively to add impact to a display. Name the children's work clearly and prominently – it is a shame to see a child pointing vaguely at a wall-display, knowing their work is up there somewhere, but unsure which of a dozen pieces of writing is theirs.

● Make sure that your own writing and labels live up to the standards you expect of your class.

● Agree mutually suitable times with another teacher to send children to show pieces of writing that they are particularly pleased with to another class. This works well between adjacent year-groups. It can also retain or forge rewarding links between a past or future teacher and classroom, providing helpful insight for teachers and continuity for children. For immediacy, such arrangements can often be planned as required during breaks.

You Can... Promote a sense of achievement

'A thing worth doing is worth doing well' as the old saying goes! It is a sentiment worth promoting from the beginning so that children develop a pride in their work and adopt an 'I can...' attitude. This is conducive to creating an atmosphere in which the children themselves expect to succeed and as a result they will gain a feeling of achievement on completion of any task.

Thinking points

● Encouraging words directed at individuals while they are working help to keep them on target and enthusiastic.

● Quiet children, who always keep on target and produce good work, may not realise how well they are doing. Keep a daily tick list alongside a register of names to ensure that everyone gets their individual pat on the back.

● Display the children's work at their eye level so that they and their peers can appreciate their achievements.

● Mount and annotate displays to show that you recognise and appreciate the children's efforts and successes.

● Keep a supply of different-coloured paper, say pink or pale yellow. Allow children who have drafted especially good work to copy it on to coloured paper as an occasional treat, highlighting their special effort.

Tips, ideas and activities

● Encourage children to keep their own records of achievement. Prepare an 'I can...' sheet for them to tick things off as they learn them. Combine practical tasks – such as ...*sharpen my own pencil, ...rule a straight line* – with cerebral tasks, such as ...*write my own name, ...leave spaces between words*, ensuring that children of all abilities can see progress.

● Exploit children's collecting instinct by giving out sticker rewards for completed achievement sheets. A sheet of ten stickers could earn the child a success celebration in school assembly.

● Allow children to decorate their best work by adding a border or coloured title or turning a story they have written into an A4 single tent-fold book.

● Ensure that the children know the purpose of their writing. They are more likely to recognise their own achievement when finished. Even for very young children, who will inevitably spend much time practising forming letters, this can become part of a larger activity, combining it with other areas of the curriculum. For example:
  ● Maths: Children practise conservation of number – sets of five letter Cs; five Os; five As; five Ds.
  ● Art and Design: Children write on gummed paper shapes to decorate objects such as a cardboard pencil holder; children practice the letter S, or words beginning with S, on a sheet of paper, then fold it into a simple origami swan.
  ● PE and games: Hold team races where each team member races to a board, writes a prescribed letter or key-word spelling, returning for the next child's turn.
  ● Geography: Children practise writing their names and add them to a classroom map showing where everyone sits.

● Finally, make the most of plenary sessions allowing children time to show or read their work aloud.

You Can... Encourage children to complete written tasks

Writing stamina, like reading stamina, develops gradually. You need to stretch children and avoid quick learners becoming bored, while avoiding over-stretching others so that they want to give up before they have begun. Striking the balance is essential if all children are to complete their writing. The thought of doing something with their writing after the activity is a useful carrot.

Thinking points

● Think about your class environment. Is there enough light in the room? Is the temperature comfortable? If it is gradually growing too hot or too dark, children will soon become lethargic.

● Ask yourself if the targets you are setting are realistic and achievable. What is a small task to one child may seem mountainous to another. Be prepared to break larger tasks down into smaller stages to make them seem more achievable.

● Have extension ideas ready for more able children so that you can allow adequate time for slower workers to complete their writing.

● Arrange for children with poor concentration to sit near the front of the class or close to you, so that they have the best chance of keeping their minds on instructions and advice.

Tips, ideas and activities

● Stopping during an activity to assess progress gives all children a break and helps to prevent enthusiasm dwindling. Hearing of someone else's progress can encourage others to keep up and give fresh direction.

● If possible, have an adult helper on hand to work with children whose attention wanders. Children who have difficulty retaining information will be more likely to complete work if they can easily check on what is required of them. Alternatively, display a numbered key-word reminder of what the written task involves, in sequence, such as: 1. Name, 2. Date, 3. Story plan, 4. Opening line.

● If the children need to copy from the board, use a different colour for each new sentence. This helps children to keep track of where they are.

● Consider an incentive at the end of a session. Children could: read out their story or poem; transfer a handwritten draft to a computer printout; illustrate their work; know that the work produced is part of an on-going project.

● Adding an extra dimension or development to their finished work offers children an incentive to complete a task. Arrange this for a separate session to prevent the children from rushing at the expense of quality. Ideas include adding their contribution to a display or turning their long thin poem into a bookmark.

● For handwriting practice, ask the children to copy out poems for display or write out menus for the dinner tables.

● Laminate children's writing to make table mats for activities using modelling clay or for snack times. They will enjoy re-reading their poems and stories and, at the end of term, each child has a preserved piece of work to take home.

You Can... Increase enthusiasm for writing

The stimulus of reading may well enthuse children to want to write, once they realise that books are written; that there is an author behind the words they read. If they enjoy reading, they may well enjoy writing, too. Young children are extremely play-oriented and will respond to any writing activity that is part of a game or can be made into one.

Thinking points

● Do children connect the name on the cover of a book or at the foot of a poem with the concept of authorship? Do they realise that people write books?

● Anyone and everyone is potentially an author – authorship is not restricted to grown-ups. Encourage the children to write a book to be added to the class library – a collection of short stories or poems by each child in the class. With spiral or heat-binders and desktop publishing this could include a front cover title and back cover blurb to make the finished product look more like a 'real' book.

● Make sure that occasionally you join in children's writing activities, so that the children see you writing too, setting an example and enjoying the creativity of the task. Share your work, along with theirs, in the plenary session.

Tips, ideas and activities

● One of the greatest incentives to get children wanting to write is to arrange a visit from an author. It helps children to conceptualise the link between reading and writing.

● Writing as a whole-class or group activity helps children to relax and enjoy the creative process while you (or adult helpers) act as scribe. Without the pressure to write themselves, they can see the process through from beginning to end. Then, when they do write for themselves, the combination of thinking and physical pencil-pushing, is easier to achieve.

● Retelling stories in their own words reduces the burden of thinking skills, enabling children to concentrate on the mechanics of handwriting, without having to be overly creative too.

● Child-centred writing helps to absorb children's interest – a diary of what they did at the weekend; writing about home and family, pets, holidays, favourite toys.

● Find ways to encourage children to read each other's writing – such as laminating and publishing the children's work to include in the book corner.

● Play writing games such as writing 'Who am I?' riddles to try out on friends.

● Ask children to think of a favourite question-and-answer joke. (Or provide joke books for children to copy from.) In groups, give each child two small pieces of different-coloured paper. On one, tell them to write the question, on the other, the answer. Then, invite them to jumble all their papers to 'mix and match'. As they read them, they must work out which is the real punchline to each joke, until they have matched all the halves correctly.

  ● Develop this another day by giving children the first half of some new jokes for them to make up funny answers to. Compare the real answers when they read out their jokes later.

You Can... **Provide building blocks to enhance writing**

If we are asked to build a house and have to learn the skills of architect, planner, site manager and bricklayer, to name but a few, it helps if, at least, the ready-made bricks are supplied. Providing building blocks is the least we can do to support early writers as they progress up their steep learning curve.

Thinking points

● Vocabulary, syntax, manual dexterity, letters, phonics knowledge, word-building and sequencing – remember that it is a huge combination of skills we expect children to learn and practise simultaneously!

● Try learning a new foreign language with unfamiliar graphic symbols and sounds and you begin to appreciate how a five-year-old child feels. However, they have quick young brains – and plenty of adult help and encouragement!

● Listen to conversations between children. Do they use many full sentences? Are they grammatically accurate? Putting full sentences together takes practice.

● Sorting is one of the most useful early activities for children when starting school and an essential forerunner to reading and writing.

● Plenty of left-to-right pattern-tracing is a good forerunner, too.

Tips, ideas and activities

● Once children recognise letters and words, they can put them together in sentences. A full sentence always involves a subject and a verb. The simplest sentence has a minimum of two words: *Jack jumped*. Try singing nursery rhymes together and create simple two-word sentences from each (noun plus verb): *Humpty sat; Mouse ran; Jill went; Jack fell*.

● As transitive verbs occur, children will realise that the sentence is bound to grow – gradually build up a two-word sentence to see how big it can grow. If we say *Lucy lost*, it sounds as if she lost a game, so we need to add an object, a noun – *Lucy lost pocket*. Children can hear that it sounds incomplete. Who does the pocket belong to? Her! So we now have a four-word sentence: *Lucy lost her pocket*. In this way the children also begin to recognise tenses –Lucy doesn't lose it; she lost it – it has already happened!

● Make up some simple sentences using verbs intransitively (for two-word sentences) or transitively (for longer sentences).

● Use the first person, *I* and *We*, to invent sentences about the school day – *I run to school. We hang up our coats.*

● Give the children jumbled sentences to rewrite. Begin with lines from familiar rhymes, such as: *Jack over candlestick the jumps*. Alternatively, use photocopiable page 56. If required, allow the children to cut up and rearrange the words, gluing them into position. Help the children to add full stops.

● Make individual sentence-makers for children to use to create simple sentences, colour-coding verbs and nouns. Protect the most common words by laminating them – individual words and personal names can be added as required. Add self-adhesive Velcro to the back of the words for use with felt-boards. This allows children to plan their sentences before writing them.

You Can... Instil confidence in spelling

Despite the diversity of English spelling there are many regular rules and conventions which help children to gain confidence. Distinguishing between vowels and consonants and counting syllables are the two most useful areas of groundwork from which to develop and refine spelling skills.

Thinking points

● 'Wunse' (as in *Wunse* upon a time) may not look right but it is a phonetically plausible and decipherable spelling attempt. Plausibility is a valid approach and valuable stage in the acquisition of spelling skills. Give it due credit and praise when marking and assessing writing.

● The letter string *b-vowel-g* offers the opportunity to use any vowel in the centre and make a real word every time! Invite the children to choose a vowel; no child will get a wrong answer – great for instilling confidence!

● Exploit the familiarity of children's own names to reinforce rules such as the softening of G and C when followed by *e* or *i*, as in George and Cilla.

● Point out that there will normally be at least one vowel in each syllable or beat of a word. For example, *mag-net; kang-ar-oo*. If they can hear and count syllables, they can begin to check for vowels.

Tips, ideas and activities

● Listen as you sound out letters. Make sure that you are not adding an extra sound. For example, the letter M says *mmm* NOT *muh*! S says *sssss* not *suh*; T, a sharp, short-tongued *t* – not *tuh*. Children sight-reading or spelling *mug* will then spell it naturally m-u-g rather than m-g. Hardest to sound correctly are B and P – barely make their sound, only parting your lips gently to avoid the extra 'uh' syllable creeping in.

● Sort the vowels from the consonants by ringing the central letter of CVC words and sounding it in isolation.

● When teaching spelling, begin with phonetically accurate words – CVC words such as *fat, get, lit*. Gradually introduce blends at the onset, beginning with the common digraphs: *sh, ch, th* and *qu*; followed by double-consonants at the end: *cuff, hill, kiss*; and common digraphs such as *ck*: *lick, back*.

● Ask children to produce spellings within centre-word vowel 'families' – *web, net, bell, mess*.

● Introduce two-syllable words where each half is a CVC component: *magnet, goblin, picnic*, and compound words: *sunset, sunhat, fishnet, piglet, zigzag, padlock, catkin*. Have fun with *Stephen*!

● Explain how *e* and *i* may soften the initial letters *c* and *g*.

● Have fun with nonsense words. These provide practice at understanding the function of vowels and their effect between consonants, without the pressure to 'spell' conventionally. Children can make up definitions to their invented words, such as *hib* – a hidden bib; *gug* – a good jug; *bogwim* – a paddle in damp grass.

● Use reading skills to reinforce written work. List sets of words and ask the children to play the role of Nonsense Detective. They must catch the nonsense word hidden in each set of words, such as:

| hid | bad | fod | bud | led | mud | did |

You Can... Support children in connecting writing to experience

Children are very much in touch with their senses, using them all to the full as they constantly try to make sense of the world around them. Every day presents new experiences and challenges for young children to absorb. Topic work that revolves around 'Myself', 'Me and My Family' and 'The Five Senses' all encourage child-centric writing possibilities, guaranteed to involve their interests and experience.

Thinking points

- There are lots of ways of linking writing to other areas of the curriculum – it might be listing things that float and things that sink under appropriate headings (science) or in sets (maths), or writing names of shapes or number words (maths), or annotating a simple map (geography).

- Use young children's natural egocentricity as a springboard for looking at others' experiences, through exploiting their imaginations. *Has anyone ever got lost in the shopping precinct? How does it feel?* and so on.

- Encourage children to voice their thoughts and share their news orally prior to writing, as it helps them to organise their thoughts and offers examples to less confident children. Inviting or asking questions as they do so will also encourage children to expand their approach to a subject.

Tips, ideas and activities

- Invite the children to draw around your hand. Inside the shape, ask them to list things that they like to touch. Encourage them to consider contrasting textures, indoors and out, at home, at school, on holiday and so on.

- Make a giant face as the centre of a wall display – link the children's writing by pinning threads of different-coloured wool from each part of the face to their lists of respective sense-related delights, adding a waving hand, for touch-related writing.

- Invite the children to bring in a photograph of themselves for 'All About Me' related writing. Topics include hobbies, favourite toys, favourite colours, pets, family and friends, and so on. Alternatively, use a digital camera and print off copies of photographs taken in the classroom.

- Link to other areas of the curriculum. For example, children could write about their athletics and games skills, timing how long they take to run around the playground or how many times they can bounce and catch a ball in one minute.

- For very young children who are practising writing their names, ask them to stick their names to different-coloured squares of paper determined by a chosen theme to fit in with topic work, such as favourite colour, food and how they came to school. Create a bar-chart from the squares.

- Ask children to write a fact file about themselves including a self-portrait, their full name and school address, their birthday, likes and dislikes, best friends, and culminating in an aspiration – *When I grow up I'd like to* (*be* or *do* or *go to…*).

- Writing personal 'news' or a 'diary' can become too much every day, but it is a worthwhile task once a week – perhaps on a Monday, when weekend activities provide subject matter.

You Can... Enhance children's writing by example and modelling

Use of the first person plural immediately involves every child, giving a sense of shared ownership and belonging. If you write a story about the children, with the children as characters in it, for example, all can contribute at an equal level. Act as scribe for the children's creative stories, demonstrating how to turn spoken ideas into written words.

Thinking points

● Using an interactive whiteboard is advantageous, as you don't need to turn your back on the children and they can see the words appear one by one, building up into sentences, with capital letters and full stops and even paragraphs.

● Shared writing is the perfect vehicle for demonstrating the drafting process inherent to nearly all writing. During shared writing you will be vocalising how, where and why to make changes, and inviting suggestions for improvement.

● During shared writing you are removing the mechanics of writing from the children, which enables them to concentrate fully on content. Perhaps surprisingly, children with literacy difficulties are often the very ones who are full of ideas!

● This kind of exercise is also an excellent forerunner to individual writing.

Tips, ideas and activities

● Planning and writing shared texts is useful for many areas of classroom life. Create a list of rules for writing, inviting suggestions from the children. Explain the need for unambiguous wording. In speech we can point and say, 'Start writing there!', but if writing the instruction we need to be more specific – *Start at the top-left of the line that is next but one after your title.*

● Look at sequencing with the children. For example, should the rule about where to start writing come before or after *Make sure your pencil is sharp?*

● Use shared writing to lead on to individual or group writing – retaining a similar theme, such as 'How to Keep Our Cloakroom Tidy'.

● Write a story together using a fantasy theme based on real-life experience, such as: 'The Day Our Classroom Flew Away'. A story like this can be used to demonstrate sentences, use of paragraphs, direct speech, inserting adjectives and changing ordinary verbs to more expressive ones. Using the children's own names helps to retain their interest and will make them want to re-read the story when it is finished.

● Ask the children to look at concrete things around them to inspire their imaginations. Ask questions such as: *What were we doing when the classroom suddenly grew wings and flew off over the playground? What happened to the paint-pots? What did we see? Where did we fly? Did we get back before home-time?*

● Allow children to write their own version of the shared story, altering names or actions as they choose.

● Encourage less able learners to sequence a series of given sentences to create a simplified version of the shared activity.

You Can... Offer strategies for effective writing

Where do I start? Any task can seem overwhelming if we don't know where to begin. As you teach approaches and strategies to effective writing you will find that not only the children benefit. Picture your favoured supermarket, walk around it in your mind's eye and write your shopping list in the order you come to the goods. It works a treat – unless the manager rearranges the shelves!

Thinking points

● Some recipes become so familiar that we can cook them without instructions, but the help of a cookery book will produce better results for more complicated recipes. The same applies to children's writing: a planning sheet helps.

● Use of writing frames breaks a writing task into manageable chunks and helps to order thoughts and planning and so to sequence sentences or paragraphs.

● Encourage the children to ask themselves questions as they write: What? Where? When? How? Why? Answering such questions automatically gives them a way into writing.

● A numbered list of key words or subtitles can help the children to order their thoughts and keep track of their progress. Remind them, though, not to use these numbers when writing unless it is an instructional text.

Tips, ideas and activities

● Most writing can benefit from the use of a writing frame. A letter can be broken up into address, greeting, main message/ purpose and closing; a story can be broken up into characters, setting and plot followed by beginning, middle, end.

● Writing instructional texts (where sequence is everything) is an easy way in to recognising how planning sentence order is imperative. Ask the children to imagine that an alien has landed from another planet and that they make friends with him and want him to go to school with them. Explain that they need to write him some instructions entitled 'How to get dressed' – What goes on first? Does a shirt button at the front or back?

● Experiment with other instructions for the alien: how to eat a bowl of cereal; how to play Tag.

● Always encourage the children to read through their work. Provide a checklist to help them:
  ● Capital letters at beginnings of sentences and names.
  ● Full stops at ends of sentences.
  ● Does it make sense?
  ● Have I missed out any words?

● Children can also begin to check their spellings – when reading through do they notice any mistakes?

● Create writing frames which can be adapted for different purposes (and made without a photocopier) by folding a piece of paper in half horizontally and then vertically before opening it out. Use the four quarters of the page to plan the order of the content with key word reminders, before writing out the full text. Number the boxes 1–4 with the number's explanation displayed for reference. For example, if the subject is a country: Box 1: Introduction: where it is; national flag and language; Box 2: weather and climate; Box 3: landscape and wildlife; Box 4: people, work, food and sports.

You Can... **Use reading and speaking skills to support writing**

The acquisition of reading and writing skills go hand in hand. The more children understand of the written word, the more they can apply their comprehension to their writing. All exposure to writing is beneficial, and the more styles and types of writing the children see, the more they will appreciate the purpose for writing. Close-reading of enlarged shared texts helps to teach basic points such as use of capitals, paragraphs, punctuation and layout.

Thinking points

● It's easy to assume that children will draw inferences from reading and apply rules to their writing. Some will, but most will need help in connecting the printed word with their own writing.

● Once children connect reading and writing, their books can be used for reference purposes when writing – for spellings and for checking whether a capital letter is needed in certain situations, and later to investigate how commas and speech marks are used.

● Many homes have no books and children may never have seen an adult reading. When the children are having an ERIC session (Enjoying Reading In Class) sit and read a book yourself (or pretend to!) so that they can see that adults read too. An occasional 'laugh aloud' during silent reading will help them to see that reading is fun!

Tips, ideas and activities

● One of the early ways into writing sentences is to recognise a sentence within text. Explain the simple rules: look for the capital letter and read to the full stop.

● Listen to children reading a shared text in a group. Ask them to take turns by stopping and changing reader at the end of a sentence.

● Invite very early writers to copy one sentence from a page of their reading book to reinforce the 'capital letter – full stop' rule.

● As children's writing skills develop, ask them to substitute single words in a sentence. For example: *Polly bought sweets*. Choose a different name and a different item: *Josh bought popcorn*.

● Develop substitution to teach specific sentence skills, such as replacing or inserting adjectives or altering verbs to be more interesting – *went* changed to *hopped, rushed, careered, raced, dawdled*, and so on.
  ● Extend such activities to suit a change of contexts. For example: *I dawdled round the supermarket; I raced to the park; I hurried to the swimming baths.*

● Play games to support sentence work, such as: *Grandma went shopping and in her basket she put some…* adding an extra item each time, and teaching (in written form) the use of commas in lists. Use the game 'The teacher's cat' to reinforce alphabetical order and to teach the purpose of adjectives: *The teacher's cat is arrogant, bold, cunning, daft*, and so on.

● Encourage children to read at home as well as at school. Introduce them to the library. Invite them to write short reviews of books as they finish reading them. Use the writing frame on photocopiable page 57 to build confidence.

You Can... Exploit child-centric writing themes

Children aged seven and under naturally have a limited experience of life and conceptual understanding of the word around them. Finding areas of interest common to most children is easy enough as long as the areas remain largely within children's experience. It is also possible to approach writing in a cross-curricular way by using themes such as Toys, Clothes, People Who Help Us, Our School, Me and My Family, Pets, and Food.

Thinking points

● Use a flow chart or spidergraph when planning a topic. You will be surprised how easy it is to incorporate several disciplines into one subject area, all involving writing.

● Encourage the children to talk about their hobbies and interests they have out of school. Listen for clues to things that will grab their enthusiasm. Try to enthuse reluctant writers with subject matter that appeals to their interests.

● Encourage reticent children to talk about aspects of school that they enjoy. Observe their play choices and achievements in the classroom and playground and draw on those for writing in the first person.

Tips, ideas and activities

● Taking Toys as a sample subject, consider how writing may develop around it, covering all areas of the curriculum.
  ● Non-fiction writing: My favourite toy – which it is; when and how I got it; why I like it.
  ● Fiction writing: 'The Lost Teddy' or 'The Magic Toy'.
  ● Science: Which toys float and which sink? Which toys break easily and why? What are the toys made of?
  ● Geography: Write about toys from different parts of the world. Do children in Norway use sledges more often than children in Britain? If so, explain why.
  ● History: Find out and write about what toys our parents and grandparents played with. Which of these are still popular today?
  ● PE: Write instructions for a new game involving hoops, beanbags or balls.
  ● Maths: Sort toys into sets and give names to the sets: bath toys; indoor toys; outdoor toys; cuddly toys. Continue by making sets of six of each type of toy.
  ● PSHE: Write rules for sharing in the classroom.

● Allow mixed-ability groups to share writing tasks according to their writing level. Tasks range from copying captions onto labels to composing and writing the results of experiments. Less confident story writers can add speech-bubble captions to graphic stories.

● Suggest that children keep an Interest Book or a Journal to which pages can be added throughout the term. Keep this essentially personal and, if possible, allow the children to keep their file to take home at the end of the term. Photocopied examples of their best work or printouts of stories keyed into the computer can be added.

● Some children will enjoy being allowed to copy out their favourite poem to add to their personal interest book or to illustrate as a poster.

You Can... Increase children's writing stamina

Just like reading stamina, writing stamina improves gradually. As the mechanics of writing become second nature, children can concentrate more on content. The desire to say what they want to say in writing will gradually supersede the simple need to comply with the requirement to complete a writing task with minimum effort.

Thinking points

● Keep targets realistic and achievable, while always having extension ideas ready for fast workers. Avoid overwhelming very young children.

● Make use of high-frequency key words that the children are used to reading. The greater exposure will help their memories when it comes to spelling these words.

● Invite children to create funny pictures in words – the desire to entertain will encourage them to increase the length of their sentence and story-writing.

● Simple captions and single words in speech bubbles are an encouraging and functional way into children's early writing experience. After retelling a story in sequential picture-boxes, speech bubbles can be written in, cut out and pasted into place.

Tips, ideas and activities

● With a group or whole class, demonstrate how to stretch simple sentences into longer, or even, complex sentences. Invite children to add adjectives, then connectives, prepositions and so on. Continue along these lines with the children suggesting words and you acting as scribe. For example, see how this four-word sentence has been stretched:

- Anna had an adventure.
- Anna had an exciting adventure.
- Brave Anna had an exciting adventure.
- Brave Anna had an exciting adventure with a crocodile.
- Gradually extend, one word at a time to: Brave Anna had an exciting adventure with a green, grinning crocodile that chased her down the river until she escaped to the bank.

● Invite the children to stretch the sentence *Bob had a ball.* Limit them to 25 words maximum (to allow for children whose writing stamina is developing beyond the scope of a reasonable sentence!). Encourage less imaginative children by asking questions, such as: *Where did Bob play with his ball? Did he throw or bounce or kick it? What happened next?*

● After the children have had some practice at stretching sentences, invite them to read some aloud. Discuss the optimum length of a sentence. Did the child need to stop and take a breath before finishing reading the sentence? If so, try breaking the sentence into two or more shorter sentences and observe how (as these all involve the same subject matter) they are creating a paragraph. Before they know it, they will be writing several sentences; more than one paragraph; a short story.

● Create cloze-procedure sentences for less confident children and offer a choice of words to slot in, for example:

Bob had a _____ ball (suggested words: *little, big, bouncy, red, blue, young, funny*) that he _____ (*threw, kicked, bounced, dribbled, hit*) right over the _____ (*hill, fence, roof, hedge, wall*).

You Can... # Develop creative play into story-writing

Watch the children in the playground. See how many different play scenarios they come up with: mums and dads; cops and robbers; competitive racing drivers, and so forth. They begin by deciding on who is playing what part (probably arguing over who draws the short straw and plays the baby in 'Mums and Dads'); then they outline a scenario, only plotting a move or two ahead before the acting begins. They are telling stories...

Thinking points

● Even before they pick up a pencil, all children are authors, just like Aesop, the Greek slave who never wrote a word in his life. Invite children to affirm this by describing some of their make-believe playground game scenarios.

● Once children recognise their creative talent, it is a small step to turning their ideas into words. Improvised drama sessions give children a chance to practise their storytelling skills. For example, two or three children might act out being indoors on a rainy Saturday – fed up with the weather and planning some game or mischief.

● Stories surround us every day of our lives – we are the chief characters in our own stories – at home, at work and in our interaction with others. These things are instant plots, characters and settings for the stories we write.

Tips, ideas and activities

● Many early readers contain stories that revolve around a domestic setting and common areas of conflict: Mum wants child to tidy room while child wants to play with friend; children fall out over sharing and have to find a way around their differences; two family members want opposing things and must reach a compromise, and so on.

● Telling stories is a great forerunner to writing them. Ask the children, in pairs, to tell each other a story. Give them a theme, such as: *The day I fell out with my brother/sister/friend; The day I couldn't stop laughing; A place I love to go; An awkward moment.*

   ● Encourage the listeners to ask one or two questions of the storytellers to increase detail and find out more.
   ● Ask the listeners to recommend a story they have listened to that others might enjoy hearing. Invite children to come to the front to retell their story, again, asking and inviting a few questions in order to elicit more detail.
   ● Ask the children to draw pictures of their story (storyboarding) to show the sequence of events as a prompt for writing.

● Provide an opening to a sentence for the children to complete to start their story. For example: *One day, when I was feeling... (bored/miserable/happy/excited)...* Discuss how the sentence is unfinished. Offer suggestions of what you might write next if you were writing your story: *...I phoned my friend and she invited me over.*

● Suggest that less confident children write a story between them, taking it in turns to physically write the next sentence, while planning the plot and wording together.

You Can... Encourage the use of brainstorming

One of the joys of creative writing is the freedom it offers. For young children whose life is dictated by adults it is a wonderful release to be in control. Characters can do things and go places that children cannot. Animals can take on human attributes and speak. Magical things like shrinking to fit inside a doll's house or a toy car or growing as tall as a house become possible. The only limit to storywriting is the child's imagination.

Thinking points

● One of the greatest blocks to creative writing is thinking too long and too hard about a plot. It is difficult to teach children to plan and yet give free rein to the imagination.

● Occasionally allowing children to do 'automatic writing' without any planning can demonstrate how restrictive over-planning can be to the imagination. Children can be amazingly responsive to the freedom of spontaneity.

● As self-expression takes off and writing stamina grows, there will be a dip in the quality of syntax, spelling and handwriting. Don't worry about this. Letting children find their creative feet will pay dividends. If their ideas flow, once they have got them down on paper, the children themselves will want to improve their transcript.

Tips, ideas and activities

● Brainstorming an idea while making notes on a spidergraph is one way of freeing up imagination and aiding lateral thinking. It's akin to a great painter's pencil sketching or an athlete's limbering up.

● Start brainstorming as a class activity, sharing ideas around a theme. A fun way to start is with a material, for example water, sand, clay, glass, chocolate. Brainstorm anything and everything associated with the material. This becomes an Ideas Bank for the children to draw upon later.

● Next, apply the same brainstorming technique to a living creature – real or mythical; human or animal. For example:
boy/girl – their likes and dislikes, home, food, clothes, lifestyle;
horse – racing horses or pulling carts and ploughs, shire horses, mythical horses; mane, tail, hooves, food, habits.

● Finally, combine a chosen material with a chosen creature to create a working title – 'The glass horse'; 'The chocolate dragon'; 'The sand cat'. Use the material that the creature is made of to suggest a plot. How will being made of sand, for example, affect the cat's life? Has it come to life when children built it on the beach? How will it fare when the tide comes in or its sand dries out? Who or what will save it from being washed away or falling into a heap?

● By working on a plot together as a whole-class activity, children learn to think widely, share ideas and choose from possible paths. They will gain confidence as they realise that there are no right or wrong answers, simply different stories.

● The children can now try to write their own version of the story. Plan the first paragraph together to start them off and to provide a model for the rest of the story.

You Can... Cultivate the notion of sharing ideas

Many of the best television sit-coms have been written by partnerships – and we're talking professional, experienced adults with a penchant and ability for writing. They know that their plotting and characterisation will improve as they bounce ideas off each other. How much more, then, will young learners benefit from sharing ideas with a partner? Two heads are often better than one!

Thinking points

- It is not recommended to force a writing partner on an independent child who is full of ideas, loves writing and whose prose flows; but for many it will encourage progress to work in twos.

- Slower writers are often creative thinkers. Consider partnering such children with quicker writers so that both benefit from sharing their skills.

- In simple terms, a story-writer is creating a linear sequence of problems and hurdles and then finding ways around them towards a satisfying ending.

- Invite an adult scribe to write down children's story plans as they tell them. Alternatively, use a sound-recorder for children to record their ideas. They can transcribe them, with help, at a later date.

Tips, ideas and activities

- Create some 'go on...' stories as a class. Start with a simple sentence: *One day, John set out for a walk when he saw a... Go on!* Choose a confident child to improvise an ending to that sentence and start a new one, repeating the story from the beginning each time: *One day, John set out for a walk when he saw a brown bear looking at him over a hedge. He was very surprised so he... Go on!* (Jot down the storyline in case of interruption or to remind the storytellers.)

  - When the children are used to this technique, organise them into twos and ask them to take turns to make up a 'go on' story with their partner. As their story starts developing, encourage them to write it down or storyboard it in pictures with brief accompanying text as reminders of the sequence of events.

  - Challenge both children in each pair to write their own version of the story. Do not worry unduly about 'copying' from each other during the writing process, as this is a shared activity and a confidence booster.

  - Allow time at the end of the session to listen to the stories. Reading their own work aloud reinforces the joy of writing and motivates the children to complete their work in the allotted time.

- If children 'dry up' on a 'go on' story, try slotting in a helping line of your own or asking an open question.

- If the children's stories become too slow-paced with too much added detail, limit them to a story in, say, 12 sentences. Tell them something very exciting must happen on or by the fourth sentence – suggest that this is either a problem that must be solved or a 'spanner in the works' – a hurdle for the main character to overcome.

You Can... Show children how to lose themselves in writing

For children, as for adults, life sometimes produces feelings of frustration, anger and sadness. Everyone has different ways of dealing with their feelings – taking solace in pets' affection, finding an outlet through sport or athletic activity. Sometimes a thumb or a cuddly toy is all that's needed, but as children get older, writing can be therapeutic. Penning their feelings can help children to deal with problems and release tensions. It can also be used to communicate unspoken feelings to others.

Thinking points

● Encouraging children to recognise and deal with their feelings will help them to cope with difficulties and channel their emotions.

● Young children can be encouraged to draw an expression inside a face to show how they feel, adding captions or speech bubbles.

● When a child is clearly upset but won't talk about the cause, suggest that they write down how they feel.

● Writing about strong feelings when the feelings are not immediately present adds distance. It provides the means to write for comfort when emotions are running high. A fictional setting further distances the writer, enabling them to write more freely.

● The irony of losing oneself in writing is that one often *finds* oneself that way too!

Tips, ideas and activities

● It is hard for young children to analyse how they feel, and why, in an abstract way. Approach feelings through concrete pictures. Begin with positive feelings of happiness or excitement. Ask the children to think of a place that they like very much – at home or on holiday, indoors or out. Invite them to tell a friend about this place, describing it in detail.

● Listen to some of these descriptions within the class. Ask questions to narrow down what is so pleasing to the child. For example, if it is his or her bedroom, what aspect makes them feel happiest – the colour scheme? Their favourite possession? The snuggly bed?

● Next, ask the children to write about the favourite place that they talked about earlier, drawing on all five senses. Ask them to imagine that something spoiled their favourite place. Explain that this is going to be the setting for a fictional story. Tell them that because they decide what happens, they, can fix it and put everything right.

● Suggest that the children write their story in the first person, without too much planning ahead. Ask them to really imagine themselves in their favourite place, in among what is happening – so much so that they forget that they are in the classroom as they lose themselves in their writing. Remind them to show how they feel through their actions and behaviour during the story's events – this could be through direct speech and the character's thoughts.

You Can... Enhance the links between reading and writing

To create a story characters, setting and plot are all needed. It is a lot to think about all at once. Help children to gain confidence by introducing these aspects gradually. They all have one familiar character, themselves – ideal for first or third person storytelling. In addition, they have familiar fictional characters that may reappear in new stories or allow them to retell traditional tales.

Thinking points

● The quality of literature the children are exposed to will influence the quality of writing they produce. Even with very young children, make sure that all the stories they encounter are well written (or well told), so that the good points are reflected in their own work.

● Children love to hear stories again and again. In your efforts to stretch their horizons, also ensure that they enjoy the comfort of familiarity through retellings of traditional tales, our shared cultural heritage.

● Ensure that the children experience stories about the same character in different scenarios, so that the character's personality and characteristic behaviour are revealed as consistent, for example Dick King-Smith's Sophie stories; Michael Bond's Paddington.

● It's easy to experiment with changing endings of familiar stories by providing printouts of a famous story (copyright permitting). Add blank lines ruled at the close for children to write their new ending.

Tips, ideas and activities

● Before children begin to write stories individually, act as scribe while they tell a story, reinforcing the connection between the spoken word and writing.

● Make up a story as a class – or retell a traditional story, such as 'Goldilocks'. Make the central character a class-member. Write the words on a whiteboard as they are created. Between sessions, transfer this to a computer. Print out copies, replacing instances of the child's name with underlined spaces. Create 'his' and 'hers' versions, replacing pronouns such as *she* with *he* or vice versa. Finally, ask the children to put themselves in the story by writing their own name in the spaces. Children find personalised stories great fun.
  ● On an interactive whiteboard, substitute different names on different days to re-read as a class. Invite children to make other word substitutions, changing verbs or adding adjectives, for example, reinforcing their function within a sentence. Recognising which word(s) cannot be changed, while retaining meaning, is as important as learning which words can.

● Invite children to choose a character they would like to meet. Plan a scenario where this could happen, for example, a new child in the class. Ask the children to choose who: Little Miss Naughty? Paddington Bear?
  ● Now invite individuals to tell the story of the new child's first day. Perhaps they had to look after the new child, but it was trickier than expected. Explain that they must draw on their knowledge of the character to think up a plot. For instance, Paddington Bear might want to keep his hat on in class or he might get marmalade on the writer's book, getting the writer into trouble. Remind the children that the character must remain 'in character' – that is, behave as they would in their original stories.

You Can... Offer children new ways into creative writing

Painting by numbers may not create artists, but it does provide experience of colour recognition and controlling a paintbrush, and there is a completed picture worth looking at by the end. Most children will not grow up to be great novelists but they can experience the fun and satisfaction of writing stories – who knows where their early efforts might lead?

Thinking points

● How often do we approach something exciting in our lives – something to look forward to – and yet at the same time have reservations or worries about it? Some are realised, many are not. From such events, great fiction can be made.

● Ask children to think of cartoons where one wild event follows another – especially Tom-and-Jerry-type humorous stories. Picturing their own story characters as in a film will help conjure ideas of 'what happens next'.

● Children are used to seeing TV stories jump from one scene to another. Ask them to picture their stories in the same way as they are planning their writing, changing scene or viewpoint as they create new paragraphs.

Tips, ideas and activities

● Play a game of 'good news/bad news'. Invent a character and plan some exciting and some worrying things that will happen to them, such as: *The good news is Katy has the chance to ride a pony. The bad news is the pony gallops before Katy is properly in the saddle. The good news is she doesn't fall off. The bad news is she gets caught on the branch of a tree. The good news is she falls into a pile of soft earth. The bad news is it's an ants' nest…* and so on.

  ● Point out that you have created a story – a string of events, each as a consequence of another. You have created problems and found solutions. All you have to do now is decide when, where and how to end your story.

  ● Discuss how the character's feelings will change as the story progresses – excited, nervous, afraid, panicky, relieved, worried, scared, amused… Think of ways this can be shown in the storytelling, beyond simply relating the bare facts and events. It can show in the character's actions, facial expressions, behaviour and speech.

● Write a story-opening together for the children to continue. Demonstrate use of sentences with appropriate punctuation. Explain that each new event can occupy a paragraph of its own. Remind children that the final paragraph must be satisfying – preferably with a happy or optimistic ending (even if the character ends up in hospital in plaster they can be 'on the mend'!).

● Use the photocopiable activity sheet on page 58 to help children to plan their own linear stories of events, plus emotions. List time-passing words and phrases to help the children to pace their stories and introduce new paragraphs, such as: *One day, Soon, After a while, The next day, Before long, Next, At last, Finally.*

You Can... Foster children's natural creativity

Most children have no problems with 'Let's pretend'! They role-play naturally in their invented games. When you read to the children you doubtless adopt a squeaky voice for a mouse and a croaky voice for a frog. Children love joining in with different voices. This is a great springboard for encouraging them to write from a different viewpoint in the third person, or in the persona of a different character in the first person.

Thinking points

● Keeping a dressing-up box in your classroom encourages children to act out different roles. It helps to develop their imaginations. It also invites interaction and suggests storylines for children to develop through natural play and improvisation.

● Also provide a collection of artefacts that suggest different characters too: a plastic sword, an eye patch, a crown, a helmet, a handbag, a plastic hammer and saw, a toy microphone, a builder's hard hat.

● If possible, keep large constructional equipment handy so that someone dressed, say, as a fire-fighter can build props (and doesn't have to extinguish the Wendy House – an unpopular move if other children are using the Wendy House for a different story!).

Tips, ideas and activities

● Display this incomplete sentence for the children to copy and complete: My name is… and I am a…. Explain that they must decide what to put in the blanks, starting with the second blank. What creature could they be? Offer and invite suggestions (anything from sea creatures to taxi drivers!). Then challenge the children to invent a name that indicate something about the character, for example: a pixie might be called Tiptoe because of how he walks, or Mr Blue Nose because of his looks, or Toady because he is often found sitting on a toadstool.

● Encourage the children to draw a picture of their character and plan how to spell his or her name. Draw attention to the use of the first person, I, in the sentence. Explain that they are going to write a story about their character as if they were the character. Say, for example: *This morning, Josh, you are Tiptoe the Pixie*, and so on.

● Encourage the children to create at least one other character to interact in their story. Ask them to create a naughty character who is causing trouble and decide how this figure tries to persuade the other character to behave.

● As the children write their stories, ask them how they are getting on – using their fictitious names and encouraging them to answer in the first person. For example: *What are you up to now, Tiptoe? Have you chased away the naughty frog yet?* This will help the children to focus on keeping their first person persona and on completing their work.

● In a separate session, when the children have finished writing their stories, put them into groups and encourage them to act out their stories in turn. Improvising dialogue will reinforce the value of direct speech in storywriting.

You Can... **Stretch children's imagination**

Children can learn from their reading that there are no limits to a writer's imagination. Applying this to their own writing opens all sorts of exciting possibilities for the imaginative child. Children with less imagination may need a little more persuasion to 'let go' and enjoy writing a fantasy story.

Thinking points

● It is often said of prolific writers, with a strongly identifiable style, that they only have one plot and their characters are always the same. Their stories may be formulaic, but they still work well as the details of place and character and setting are different every time.

● *First, Then, Next, Lastly…* sums up the stages of a simple story. It also offers a ratio for introduction, middle and end – useful for infant story writers.

● Introducing fantasy elements into a story forces the imagination to stretch, so even an everyday setting can become fantastic and extraordinary.

● Sometimes it's good to work together as a class or in a group until children's confidence builds up and they are ready to attempt writing on their own.

Tips, ideas and activities

● Themes occur again and again in stories from different sources and different authors. How many story characters can you think who are gullible or unprotected and are tricked by someone mean or mischievous? Cinderella; Snow White; Little Red Riding Hood, to name but a few! Usually, revenge and/or championing of the innocent is the outcome.

● Practise simple deconstruction of familiar stories with the children to determine the three components of a story: setting, character(s) and plot. For example:
  ● Setting – two cottages at either side of a forest
  ● Characters – main characters: Little Red Riding Hood, Wolf; other characters essential to the plot: Woodcutter (Dad), Grandma; lesser character: Mum
  ● Plot: Girl sets out on errand for Mum to deliver cake to Grandma; warned not to stop and to speak to strangers; girl disobeys warning – picks flowers and talks to wolf. On arrival at Grandma's, girl is fooled into thinking wolf in disguise is Grandma – almost gets eaten alive. Dad comes to rescue with axe and Grandma is found locked in cupboard in her vest!

● Ask the children to think of all the different settings they can from the real world and then add any made-up places and worlds – these are beyond counting. The number of different potential characters is equally infinite, especially if one counts animals acting like humans, and inanimate objects coming to life. The variation of plot is also infinite – although themes will occur again and again, the details will differ.

● Give the children dice and copies of photocopiable page 59 to come up with components for a story. Allow them to work in pairs to plan how one character will trick another and how the fooled character will win through with the help of a third.

You Can... **Take the fear out of writing**

Lack of information and concern about failure are two causes of fear about writing. The more information you offer in terms of structure and materials, the better equipped the children will be and the more likely they are to have confidence, and enjoy and improve their writing.

Thinking points

● The writer's materials are not so much pencil and paper as ideas, words and sentences. It is possible to provide prompts for all these.

● Writing the most basic of stories can be practically as simple as 'joining the dots'. If the dots are in place, there's scope for the children to make their joining lines more decorative and exciting on the way.

● Story writing is one of the easiest exercises in which to provide differentiation within a mixed-ability or mixed-age group.

● Provide a solid structure to encourage even the most diffident young writers to give it their best shot.

● When providing lists of supportive text for story-writing such as joining words, time phrases, numbers and so on, use different coloured inks or card for ease of identification and reference.

Tips, ideas and activities

● The notion of a story following a timeline – a sequence of cause-and-effect events, has already been explored. Reinforce this by presenting just such a structure as 'pegs' on which children can hang each story stage. Try the following seven-sentence or seven-paragraph story. The character's name can be changed or children can write about themselves:

  ● One Monday morning something happened that made me feel… (worried/surprised/happy/angry).
  ● By Tuesday, things had changed…
  ● On Wednesday afternoon…
  ● It was Thursday when…
  ● Things got worse on Friday…
  ● At last, it was Saturday and…
  ● Finally, first thing on Sunday…

Discuss possible events that could cause a change of mood. Explain that, each day, something else must happen – sometimes good, sometimes bad. On Sunday, everything is sorted out and the story has a happy ending.

● Alternatively, provide a set of pictures that tell a simple story using stickmen figures. For example: 1. Child playing in garden with kitten chasing string. 2. Dog comes through open gate, chases kitten up tree. 3. Child closes gate and leans plank against tree. 4. Kitten descends to proffered saucer of milk. Encourage the children to sort the pictures into logical order and choose character names before writing the story.

● Write up a choice of opening lines for the children to copy to 'warm up' their pencils: *Once upon a time*; *One day*; *Not so long ago…*

● It is always easiest to write about what you know. Think about children's experiences in their daily lives. Use implicit conflicts as story titles to suggest a plot: The Lost Pet; No Party Invitation; Late for School; The Wobbly Tooth. Advise children to keep asking and answering questions if they get stuck: Who? Why? What? How?

You Can... **Facilitate children's self-expression**

It's not uncommon to walk into a classroom and think children are practising meditation techniques as they chant various mantras: 'Full stop, capital letter'; 'And is banned'; 'There's no such word as can't'. But if such mantras are hammering away inside children's heads, it may just remind them to apply some of these rules. My own addition would be, 'Keep reading it aloud!'

Thinking points

● Mistakes that are not immediately obvious visually, leap to the attentive ear of any writer who reads their work aloud.

● Reading the written word aloud is a fail-safe way of achieving rewrites and improvements without it seeming a chore. Instead of its becoming a separate activity, it is simply a part of the whole writing process.

● I believe it is only lawyers who omit commas to avoid confusion or misinterpretation. For the rest of the world, a carefully positioned comma works towards clarification. Consider the difference punctuation would make to the following, unpunctuated, sentence: *Although John swam like a fish out of water he got little exercise.* (Although John swam like a fish, out of water he got little exercise.)

Tips, ideas and activities

● Punctuation is the most useful tool towards comprehension – both recognising it in a pause when reading, and applying it when writing.

● Children do not need to know the word 'clause' to appreciate that some parts of compound sentences carry less weight than the main part.

● Write the following sentence for the children to read: *Jack put his gloves in his pocket and, swinging his bag over his shoulder, he set off down the road.* Ask the children to picture what is happening in this short, one-sentence scene. There are three things. Together, create three short sentences from the longer one: *Jack put his gloves in his pocket. Jack swung his bag over his shoulder. Jack set off down the road.*

  ● Which do the children think carries the story forward? Arguably, it would be Jack's progress down the road. Read the three short sentences aloud, then the compound sentence again, pausing briefly at each comma. Explain how the latter flows better. Show how the commas separate the three ideas within the one sentence.

● Ask the children to find and copy a long, compound sentence from a book. Advise them to look for a sentence that contains commas. Challenge them to work out what is the main, most important, part of the sentence. How many small, simple sentences can they create from the longer one?

● Finally, give the children further groups of two or three short, simple sentences from which they should create a longer, compound sentence, using commas to aid clarity. Encourage them to read their sentences aloud, pausing at the commas. Check that the commas are in the right places to make sense.

You Can... **Establish the value of drafting**

If a thing's worth doing, it's worth doing well. Drafting is particularly important with poetry where every word carries weight and is of equal importance to its neighbour. Lines must sound right, look right and, above all, make sense – so it will take some skill and practice. Children aren't afraid of poetry, so don't you be!

Thinking points

● Young children love rhythm and rhyme. Exploit their pleasure and enjoy these poetic attributes with them.

● Let children walk before they learn to run. They have the rest of their life to learn about non-rhyming and prose-poems. Let them enjoy the many rhymes and near-rhymes that the English language offers.

● Although the shape of poems on the printed page is important, poetry cries out to be read aloud. Bring it to life whenever you can.

● Learning by heart is a gift for the children to enjoy for the rest of their lives. My mother in her late eighties can still recite poems learnt at infant school, giving her great pleasure and delight to this day!

● When you plan a poetry writing activity, always start and finish with the rewarding sharing of this very aural form: read a poem – write a poem – read a poem!

Tips, ideas and activities

● There is a wealth of child-friendly traditional, ancient and modern rhymes on every subject. Recite some with the children repeatedly until the rhythms become instinctive.

● Pick a simple rhythm as a structure for children's own writing both to challenge and reassure them as they begin to play with words. See photocopiable page 60 suitable poems.

● Collect thematic words or objects to sort according to syllable count – sticking to one- or two-syllable words. For example, mini-beasts (use plastic models to sort!): ant, fly, moth, bee, snail, slug (all fairly easy to rhyme); spider, cockroach, beetle, housefly, hornet.

  ● Invite the children to select appropriate words to finish the lines, introducing rhymes as in the original. For example:
  One for a hornet,
  Two for a bee,
  Three for a housefly,
  Buzzing round me.

  ● The drafting process comes into play as together you create the fourth line in each stanza. Children may come up with several ideas – *The housefly wants to eat my tea*; *It keeps buzzing around my head*, and so on. Adapt these to fit the rhythm while retaining the meaning – *Three for the housefly that wants to eat my tea/that's landed in my tea/that is sitting in my tea…* already there are choices in terms of meaning, choice of rhyme and adapting syntax to suit rhythm – note how *that is* and *that's* are used in different options. Explain how to lose or gain a syllable to retain the rhythm. Keep reading aloud and clapping the rhythm to check what works.

  ● Having modelled how to draft, let the children have a go in pairs or small groups, attempting a second stanza or writing a new poem to link with topic work.

You Can... Engender children's belief in their own ability

Poetry is all about words – choosing the very best words and arranging them in the very best order. Children will hear and recognise rhymes, indeed, they will provide them if you stop short when reading a poem aloud. Thinking up rhymes and recognising how best to position them is harder. Work with what the children can learn easily and the rest will follow in time.

Thinking points

● By experimenting with poetic devices in isolation, children begin to build up a box of tools to draw upon when they write their own poems.

● Playing with rhythm, rhyme and alliteration is not only fun, it increases children's phonological awareness, so that all their literacy skills benefit.

● Encouraging children to clap rhythms will help them to recognise how to adapt language for poetry.

● Working with rhyme provides useful phonic recognition, reading and spelling practice – a handy spin-off when learning how to handle one of English poetry's most recognised devices.

● Children will encounter repetition in many infant poems. By practising creating repetitive refrains, children also practise repeating spelling patterns, reinforcing phonic awareness. By the time children have written *Bang, bang, bang!* their confidence and belief in their own ability has increased.

Tips, ideas and activities

● Demonstrate how to create rhymes by looking at the end sound of the starter word – *end*, itself, for example. Experiment with consonants in front: *b-end, m-end*. Children with a sharp ear may offer multi-syllable words: *off-end* and words with onset-digraphs: *bl-end, tr-end*. Write suggestions in two colours, separating onset and rhyme. Remember that as long as children's suggested words do rhyme, they have succeeded in their task and deserve praise. Asking them to create real words is a separate task. They will soon combine the two.

● Challenge groups to create as many different rhymes as they can within five minutes. Limit them to real words when you feel it is appropriate. Gradually, extend rhyme-finding beyond CVC words and extend to same sound, different spelling: *aw, or, ore, our*, for instance. Avoid endings fraught with danger such as *-uck*!

● Follow this up with exercises using other poetic devices. Children are quick and responsive practitioners of alliteration. Begin simply by linking adjectives to nouns: *bouncy ball, burst balloon; soft silk*.

● Choosing S and B exemplifies the use of alliteration in poetry – pleasing to the ear, while performing another function – the repeated soft S reinforces the softness of the subject matter. The abruptness of B exaggerates and emulates the bounce of the ball and the pop of the balloon – overlapping with another poetic device, onomatopoeia (when a word sounds like its meaning – *bang* and *splash* for example).

● Use photocopiable page 61 in part or as a whole, depending on age, ability and what you want children to practise. The sheet doubles up as an assessment and self-assessment resource, so children are able to recognise their own learning achievements. Use correction fluid or sticky notes to adapt the sheet, allowing reuse with the same group, for you and the children to monitor progress.

You Can... Motivate creative writing

Poetry is a versatile medium for writing. Through it we can express emotions and deep thoughts or tell a story or use wordplay for humour – and everything in between. There is almost nothing that cannot become the subject of a poem. This might explain why every poet you meet will have often been told: 'You could write a poem about that!'

Thinking points

● Whatever the style, whatever the subject matter, collecting thoughts, ideas, information and useful words and phrases, has to be a forerunner to drafting and crafting a poem.

● Poems feed on all fives senses, so a sensual stimulus is a great way to start a poem – a touch, a sound or a taste.

● Children's personal experience will provide the best material, so encourage them to think about their own lives and concerns when writing.

● Join in with the children, making up your own poem. You will gain experience first hand, and realise the children's dilemmas, while also showing them that poetry is not an activity just for school or children – anyone can have a go.

Tips, ideas and activities

● Ask the children to imagine themselves somewhere they love, perhaps on holiday, or a favourite place at home, say, in the bath. Ask them to close their eyes and 'listen' in their minds for what they can hear – gulls calling; a train whistle; waves shushing on the shore; bubbles fizzing. Repeat with other senses – the taste of salt in the air; icecream on the tongue; the feeling of sand running between fingers; the sight of kites diving in the sky; the smell of seaweed or bath salts.

   ● Encourage the children to list their experiences under the five senses headings. This is the raw material which they will put into their poem. Give them a simple structure. This could be as little as *I see...* as the opening of each line, followed by a noun and a verb in the present participle, for the first stanza; with the second stanza following the same pattern, but beginning, *I hear...*
   For example:
   I hear children cheering,
   I hear gulls calling,
   I hear waves crashing,
   I hear donkeys hee-hawing.

   ● As children create their simple verses, challenge them to create a repetitive refrain that talks about their chosen place, to sit between the verses, such as: *On the beach, along the sands; On the beach at Blackpool.*

● Help less creative children to adapt others' ideas, or provide a stanza and refrain for them to use as a model.

   ● See photocopiable page 60 for model poems with simple structures or find other simple-structure poems to use as examples. Try using the 'Daffodil Dip' poem on page 60: *Out* and *it* or *on* all offer plenty of rhymes, so children can begin, *Dip, dip,* and follow with the da-di-da, da, da, da, rhythm. For example:
   Dip, Dip, come and go, here and gone,
   Dip, dip, come and go, you are on.

You Can... Create and provide resources

Thesauruses and rhyming dictionaries are a great asset to any poetry writer. Even if the children are not ready to use a thesaurus by themselves, having one for your own reference is useful. Using a thesaurus will help you to help the children to avoid clunky phrases as they rewrite draft poems while retaining the essence of what they want to say. They can begin to use children's rhyming dictionaries, although it is fun thinking up rhymes for themselves.

Thinking points

● Display an alphabet chart where every child can see it easily, or have individual alphabets in front of each child. Working systematically through the alphabet speeds up rhyme searches. Mark vowels in a different colour so that children know to skip these in preference for consonants when they are searching for onset sounds of rhyming words.

● For purposes of rhyme searches, it also helps to tack *ch*, *sh*, and *th* to the end of the alphabet – or opportunities to use these sounds may be missed.

● Often, children looking for alliterative phrases will turn to a dictionary. Make sure that dictionaries are easily accessible for individual and spontaneous use.

● Remind children using alliteration that it is the sound, not the letter, that counts: *jolly giraffe*; *clever chameleon*; *chunky chocolate*; *singing cicada*, and so on.

Tips, ideas and activities

● As you teach phonics in the early years, create loose-leaf sheets of words which can be filed to create your own class rhyming dictionary. Keep short vowel rhymes in alphabetical order at the beginning of your file; long vowel sounds following. Add index dividers for ease of reference.

● Create a poetry corner in your classroom with easily accessible poems to read. Find ways for children to read poems without even opening a book.

● Make large cubes from thick coloured card to keep on the floor in a carpeted area. Paste a different poem on each face of the cube. (Stuff screwed-up newspaper inside each cube to strengthen its life). Children enjoy turning to each fresh face to read the poems.

● Similarly, create an A4 concertina book to keep on the carpet. Laminate individual pages before hinging them together with sturdy tape to extend their lifespan.

● Scatter some cushions among your poetry resources to encourage children to sit and read.

● The more poetry children read, speak and listen to, the more their writing will improve. As rhythms and structures become ingrained in their memories, so they build up a personal, mental resource of patterned language to emulate.

● Set up a rhyme table and allow the children to add items to it: *hat, cat, bat, mat, Postman Pat* and so on.

● Get a rhyming dictionary of your own – more expansive than those for children's use. It will increase your confidence when modelling the writing of rhyming poetry.

● If you are writing poems on a specific theme, such as dragons, create a word-bank of useful words: scales, tail, fly, cave, guard and so on. Using different coloured inks helps children to locate a spelling.

You Can... **Broaden the appeal of writing**

Poems can serve more than one purpose, and riddles are a poetic form that invites thought and comprehension in both the reading and the writing. When the children have written riddles, their classmates will have extra motivation to listen to their performances as they try to guess what is hidden in the words. Turning writing into a game immediately broadens the appeal.

Thinking points

● If we pick up a pencil and try to draw something it can be quite difficult, even for someone artistic. If the thing we are aiming to depict is in front of us, to study, examine and copy, it becomes easier. The same applies to writing poetry. Descriptions improve if children can look closely at their subject, and notice all the aspects of it.

● Poems are intended to be read aloud. Riddles encourage children to listen closely.

● Build up a class collection of riddles for the children to look at when they want to – once hooked, children may even want to have a go at writing some in their own time to bring to school and show to the class the next day.

Tips, ideas and activities

● A 'Who am I?' style riddle requires descriptive writing and requires some knowledge of, or the chance to closely observe, the subject matter.

● Read the riddles in the poem on photocopiable page 60. Can the children guess what each is about? Display the poem and discuss the structure and layout. Note how the first three lines of each stanza describe the creature – adopting the first person; writing in the persona of the butterfly or snail – and how both last lines begin *Who am I who...* followed by a verb. Determine which words and phrases provide the strongest clues.

● Make up a new riddle as a whole-class activity. Perhaps pick an inanimate object in the classroom, say, a book. Explain that you don't want to give away the answer in the first line. For example: *Turn my pages, read my words*, immediately gives the answer... whereas, *Hard shell on the outside, Black and white inside,* doesn't.
  ● Initially, ask the children to consider meaning, direct and concealed, and rhythm rather than rhyme. On redrafting, rhymes could be introduced. Clap the rhythms of the poems, checking that lines are not too long.

● Invite children to write their own riddle following the structure practised together. The natural world offers huge variety – the moon, a puddle, a lion, an ant. If children are short of ideas, write a few suggestions on slips of paper for them to think about, without others hearing. Include other related key words to help less confident writers. Remind them that they must not use the item's name – the answer – in the writing.

● Encourage the children, when reading their riddles aloud, to pause briefly at the end of each line, accentuating the rhythm. Ask listeners not to call out answers but raise their hand if they want to guess. Ask how they solved the riddle.

You Can... Maximise the versatility of poetry

One of the joys of writing poetry is the freedom it offers. As with story writing, infant poets can choose who to be, where to go, what to do – limited only by their imaginations. The difference is that in poetry they will demonstrate their choices within a structure of patterned language.

Thinking points

● Simple structures give confidence, but nevertheless allow children lots of scope for imaginative thinking.

● The best structures for very young children's early poems offer natural differentiation for mixed-ability groups.

● A basic recognition of nouns, verbs and adjectives will help children to adapt their language to a set structure. If they can see that each line begins with, say, a noun, this will help them to choose appropriate words to retain the pattern.

● Poetry reading and writing provides the perfect platform for enriching a child's vocabulary, through finding synonyms to express an idea or a word-picture in the best way.

Tips, ideas and activities

● Create a set of flash cards of prepositions and prepositional phrases (using capitals for onset letters if you want the children to write to a traditional format): *Up, Down, Through, Beside, Along, Between, Into, Out of, Below, Above, Over, Under, Around, Against, Towards, With, Inside, Among.*

● Read them with the children, asking them to demonstrate the meaning of each one, using their hands and fingers to show how relative place is described by each word.

● Tell the children that you are going to set off on a journey. It could be an exciting, adventurous or magical journey – or whichever adjective you choose. Explain that the journey will take the form of a poem where every line of each stanza begins with a preposition from the flash cards.

● Copy one word onto a whiteboard, for example, *Along*. Ask the children for suggestions of where they could be moving along: *Along a path; Along the river; Along a tightrope.*

● Before selecting and writing the end of the line, ask the children to tell you something more about the path, river or tightrope – ask for adjectives. Look for alliteration as well as meaning – a *pebbly path*; *rapid river*; *terrifying tightrope* and so on.

● Write the children's favourite choice, briefly discussing why it appeals, and now add the pronoun *we* followed by a verb (in whichever tense you are practising):

● *Along the pebbly path we race...* (present tense)

● *Along the rapid river we rolled...* (past tense + added alliteration)

● *Along the terrifying tightrope we wobbled...* (meaning suggesting action)

● Carry on adding lines in four-line stanzas, either as a class, in groups or as individuals. Challenge the children to bring their poem to a climax – perhaps with a fantasy element – to escape the dragon's jaws or – for humour, an anticlimax – to get to school on time!

You Can... **Use speaking games as a writing stimulus**

Lists are a big part of daily life – shopping lists, to-do lists, things to bring to school lists – this list of lists itself begins to sound like a poem in the making! Then there are lists on your classroom wall: days of the week, months of the year, a list of children's names in the register. We are surrounded by them. A number of speaking games revolve around lists – why not use lists to have some fun with words?

Thinking points

● Have a look through some of the numerous poetry anthologies available – you will soon find lots of sample 'lists' poems.

● Lists are very flexible – one or two words per line, and you have a long thin poem; or they can be written as rhyming couplets with a few more words per item. Use *number plus other adjective plus noun* for a simple format that is easy to work with.

● Most ideas can be adapted to link with topic work or themes. Imagine how much the children would enjoy performing their own original poem in a class assembly – and how proud you would feel of their efforts!

Tips, ideas and activities

● Play the game 'Grandma went shopping'. Children take turns to repeat the opening line, adding an item, and trying to remember what went before, so that the list grows. (Scribble the list as you go!)

● Take the list of items in Grandma's basket. Write the first four on the board:
Grandma went shopping and in her basket she put…
A bag of apples
A loaf of bread
Sausages
Toilet paper

● Explain to the children that you want to know more about each item. What did the apples look or feel or smell like? Take suggestions, and draft a model line: *A bag of apples, crisp and green.*

● Do the same with the next item, only, this time, make a rhyming couplet with the previous line. So, before asking for ideas about the bread, make a rhyme-bank by collecting some -*een* rhymes.

● Remind the children that these rhymes will describe the loaf of bread. Explain that all are good rhymes, but some are more useful than others. *Mean* doesn't sound too helpful. But its crust might have a nice *sheen*; is it the biggest loaf ever *seen* or fit for a *queen*? Experiment with phrasing, reading aloud and looking for rhythm and meaning. Do the same with the next two items, extending them into another rhyming couplet.

● Challenge the children in pairs to write a couplet for the remaining items. Form all the couplets into a class poem. Keep a four-line stanza layout. Adapt the opening line for the poem's title:
In Grandma's Shopping Trolley
A bag of apples, crisp and green,
A loaf of bread, fit for a queen,
Sausages waiting to sizzle and pop,
Toilet paper, the best in the shop…

● Perform it as a class, enjoying the rhythm and rhymes.

You Can... Increase children's sense of ownership

Putting the children in a poem is great fun, Most, if not all, children will love to be in their unique class poem and will want to read, recite and perform it again and again. It's a great way of ensuring everyone's enthusiastic involvement in the writing process.

Thinking points

- This exercise practises and demonstrates rhyme, rhythm, alliteration, word order and meaning, rhyming couplets, use of diminutives (as names are sometimes contracted), use of the apostrophe, proper nouns and verbs, refrains (optional), as well as providing another opportunity to demonstrate the drafting process: that's a lot of ticks in a lot of literacy boxes!

- Wait four years and ask your children if they remember any poems from their time in your class. I guarantee many will remember this one simply because they were in it. In fact, they will probably tell you it was their favourite!

- Children reluctant for their name to be used can adopt a pretend friend – an invisible new boy or new girl in the class. Or they might prefer to use a middle name.

amble - scramble - bounce - flounce - catch - scratch - cry - fly - cook - look - care - glare - dance - glance - hop - lop - huddle - cuddle - jump - bump - kick - lick - like - bike - mix - fix - gnaw - saw - peep - sleep - leap - weep - queue - chew - race - pace - trace - skate - wait - slide - ride - hide - type - wipe - wake - bake - yell - sell - tell - zoom - boom

Tips, ideas and activities

- Collect verbs including some that rhyme (see the box below). Check that you have at least one verb beginning with the same sound as each child's name. Explain that the children are going to put themselves into a poem.

  - Firstly, they must find a verb that not only describes something they could do, but begins with the same sound as their name. Emphasise *sound*, not *letter*! For example, Chloe could climb, but not chew; Charles could chew but not cook! Allow children whose names begin with a vowel to pick a prominent consonant in their name, so Oliver could have *leap*, *vote* or *love*.

  - Demonstrate how to use the present participle in a simple sentence: *Billy is bouncing*. Ask the children to say their alliterative line aloud.

  - Ask others to raise their hand if they think that their line rhymes. Write rhyming couplets to demonstrate end-of-line rhymes. Show how rhythm can be improved sometimes by the use of apostrophes. Gradually extend the class poem:
  Billy's bouncing
  Fay is flouncing
  Kim is catching
  Simin's scratching

  - Read the class poem aloud together and adjust any rhythmic glitches.

  - Challenge children to create a chorus such as: *In Class Two/Guess what we do…*

- In a separate session, consider extending the short couplets into longer rhyming couplets. Ask questions to elicit ideas, such as: *Where is Billy bouncing? What is Kate catching?*
  Billy's bouncing all across the floor,
  Fay is flouncing out through the door.
  Kim is catching the mouse her mother fears
  Simin is scratching it behind its ears.
  (This also demonstrates internal rhymes, which the original verbs have become.)

You Can... Persuade children to speed up their writing

It's easy for young children to lose sight of the wood for the trees! They can easily forget the purpose of their writing if they spend too long over it. Able writers who are enthusiastic will probably crack on quickly, but others will need a combination of practical help and added incentives.

Thinking points

● Lighten the load of copying by providing a skeleton poem, a cloze procedure where children only have to think about how they will personalise a poem within a structure.

● Motivation can come in many forms, but it needs putting in place ahead of the activity, with reminders during the activity to sustain steady progress.

● Walking around the class making audible observations of admiration at the amount written will help spur on others to impress you equally.

● Daydreamers, easily distracted from the task, may benefit from sitting in smaller groups or with one-to-one adult help until they develop concentration skills.

Tips, ideas and activities

● Begin and end poetry writing activities with poetry reading. The form demands to be read aloud and reminds children what they are aiming at. Announce in advance that only children who have finished their poem (or at least their first draft – giving you leeway for discretion and differentiation!) will be permitted to perform their poem at the end of the session.

● Provide slower workers with a writing buddy. Allow them to take it in turns to perform the physical process of writing while also sharing ideas and planning.

● When drafting early stages of a poem or brainstorming ideas, set tight time limits and 'pencils down' orders before listening to results. This sets the tone for speed from the outset and promotes faster thinking processes.

● Create a further stage of development, beyond the physical writing, that only those who have finished will be allowed to do. For example:

　● Allow children to write a fair copy of their poem inside appropriately shaped templates.
　● Offer children the opportunity to illustrate their poem when it is finished and neatly written.
　● Create a 'thank you' poem to go inside a greetings card or a Mother's Day card ready for an occasion when it's needed.
　● Write a poem about a festival to hang on a tree. (A branch sprayed silver and embedded in a large, sand-filled plant pot also works well.) Have handy appropriate shapes – eggs, stars, baubles and rockets, as well as a hole-punch and lengths of coloured wool.

● The immediacy of such display is incentive in itself. As quicker workers finish their poem and help in the display process, slower writers are motivated to complete their work in order to join in. However, ensure that some follow-ups involve all children, fast and slow alike.

You Can... Increase children's confidence

Children's confidence comes from knowing what is expected of them, combined with the knowledge that they can do it. The oral element of poetry lends itself to choral speaking and allows every child to join in however diffident they may be as a solo performer. Occasionally giving girls and boys the chance to perform as separate groups helps you to watch for anyone not joining in. It also exploits natural rivalry to motivate children to make their best effort.

Thinking points

● When reading poems with the children, remember to pause before rhymes and choruses, allowing children time to provide the rhyme or join in with the chorus.

● When writing remind them that they will need to combine sound with meaning.

● Expose the children to a wide variety of styles of writing, but keep coming back to the old familiar and popular poems, too. It encourages children to learn by heart and gives them poems to remember and enjoy all their lives.

● Make sure you include plenty of poems with actions and finger rhymes. The multi-sensory approach enhances learning and increases confidence.

Tips, ideas and activities

● Working from the known to the new increases confidence. Counting poems are always a good start for children's own writing. Traditional rhymes such as 'Five Little Speckled Frogs' and 'Ten Little Teddy Bears' offer boundless possibilities.

  ● Recite the originals with the children until the pattern and rhythm become second nature. Now, begin to take suggestions for substitutions – *Six spotty spiders hanging from a tree...* and so on. Work orally before asking the children to write their new verses.

  ● Don't forget verses that count up as well as down, such as 'One, two, buckle my shoe'. Number words all provide plenty of rhymes – for example: *One, two, a plateful of stew; three, four, a hammer and saw...*

● Teach the rhyme about the wind on photocopiable page 60.

  ● Adapt it to other aspects of the weather, asking the children to think of ideas, such as: *When the rain beats on the wall...* (*Then I cannot bounce my ball* or *All the snails begin to fall*). Practise placing the rhyme word at the end of the line. Ask the children in pairs or individually to try the following (sample rhymes in brackets):

  ● *When the rain falls on the trees...* (breeze, knees, sneeze, bees, wheeze, freeze, cheese, threes)

  ● *When the rain falls on the sea...* (me, tea, be/bee, free, three)

  ● Alternatively, make it a little harder by not providing a rhyme bank, and giving the children more choice of line ending:

  ● *When the sun shines on our...* heads/town/school/flowers

  ● *When the snow lies on my...* hat/nose/shoe/bike

● This exercise can be adapted to topics other than weather, such as family:

  ● When my mum comes home at three/four/five/six...

  ● When my dad goes to the shops/off to work

  ● When my brother/sister plays with me

You Can... **Help children to write more thoughtfully**

Poems are a classic outlet for the expression of feelings. Allowing children to write down how they feel will not only help them to feel better, but also serve to communicate their feelings to others. Writing can defuse a build-up of sadness, anger or frustration, but it can also be a celebration of happiness and joy.

Thinking points

● Children's moods can swing from elation to tears quite rapidly, especially if it is an exciting time of year, or if they are coping with grief in their personal lives. As children begin to recognise their feelings, writing can channel their emotions creatively.

● Collect examples of poems that express emotions. Read them to the children. Make sure that there is a balance of happy and sad poems as well as poems that offer excitement or, conversely, quieter, thoughtful sentiments.

● When a child is clearly upset but won't say why, suggest that they write down how they feel. Allow them to keep this private unless they invite you to read it.

● If a child discovers a poem that touches them, allow them to copy the poem out to keep. It could form the nucleus of a personal anthology of favourite poems or a class anthology of 'Poems about Feelings'.

Tips, ideas and activities

● Demonstrate that poems that touch on feelings are not necessarily 'about' feelings in terms of subject matter. For example, Robert Louis Stevenson's poem, 'The Swing' (see photocopiable page 60) is a very happy poem, describing the delight of swinging. At no point does the poet use the word 'happy', but children will recognise how the child in the poem is feeling.

  ○ *Ask, Does anyone enjoy swinging at the park or in their garden? What views do you see? Do you have a wall, a fence or hedge that you can see over?*

● Ask the children to describe an activity that makes them feel very happy or carefree. These might include swimming, scooter or skateboard riding, horse-riding, cycling, baking cakes, dipping into a crisp new comic, visiting a toy shop, cuddling a pet. Encourage children to pick participatory activities rather than sedentary activities such as watching TV.

  ○ Ask them to write a sentence about what it is like when they are pursuing their enjoyable activity. Experiment with paraphrasing some of Stevenson's poem in more modern language – say, *Guess what it's like to…*, rather than *How do you like to…?*
  ○ Continuing to use the original poem as a model, what other word could replace *pleasantest* – itself an unusual superlative? Perhaps the *wickedest* thing; the *brilliantest* thing?

● In a separate session, ask the children to write a likes and dislikes poem – begin with dislikes, introducing a contrasting 'like', such as:
I don't like thunder,
I don't like clouds,
But I do like puddles
And splashing in my boots.

● Demonstrate to the children how their poems can prove true the old maxim 'Every cloud has a silver lining', steering each verse to a positive ending!

You Can... Invite children to enjoy each other's writing

In any creative environment, people benefit from sharing each other's work. Ideas bounce off each other and develop in different, personal ways. Writers of any age will be influenced by what they read and hear and by what their peers write. It is sometimes hard for children to realise that this is not necessarily conscious 'copying'. Where children do feel proprietorial about their ideas, impress upon them that they should be flattered if their work inspires others. Poetry, especially, benefits from being performed.

Thinking points

● Practising voice projection is always useful before any reading – whether in class or in a hall. It is equally important to ensure that listeners are silent and still.

● Standing up and facing the audience is important if others are to hear a child read. Preferably invite children to the front of the class to avoid the listeners growing restless if they can't hear. This will also help to focus the other children's attention.

● Allowing children to read in groups increases their confidence, even if they still read individually within the group.

● In larger rooms or a hall, arrange a safe plinth for readers to stand on – just high enough to raise the reader's height and help a small voice to carry.

Tips, ideas and activities

● A follow-up plenary session is a useful time to share aloud what the children have written. If they have put a lot of effort into their work it is greatly rewarding to be able to share and enjoy each other's success. Children can be shy about reading their own words to others – especially if their writing is none too legible. Be on hand to help them out if they get stuck.

● Get children used to reading aloud from familiar printed texts first. These can be favourite poems from anthologies or collections. Remind them to read more slowly than they would in their heads to allow the audience to listen. (Listening to poems without the words in front of you takes practice, too.)

● Encourage children to learn the words of a poem by heart so that they can look at their audience when they recite the poem.

● Consider opportunities for children to read their poems aloud; firstly, within their own classroom; next, to another class; finally, in assembly. Link poems to a theme for an assembly.

● Create visual ways for children to share their poems with a wider audience, for example, poetry posters or a dedicated poetry page in the school newsletter.

● Ask children to vote for their favourite poem after reading and listening to each other's poems. Print the poems and give each child a sticky-note voting slip to attach anonymously to the page of their favourite. Don't allow them to vote for their own! Display the winner's poem in pride of place. (A simple frame, without glass, pinned to the wall will give the chosen poem due prominence.)

● Record an audio tape of children reading their own poems. With accompanying printed text it makes a valuable classroom resource, highlighting both written and oral aspects of poetry.

You Can... **Provide a role model**

There's nothing like a visit from a professional children's poet to inspire your children. A performance will bring life to the printed word – as will a new voice and a fresh face. Children can ask questions on the writing process, enjoy a workshop and realise that writing is not just something teachers make them do. A visiting poet acts as an advocate for writing and a role model for the writer.

Thinking points

● Plan what you want from the day before inviting your visiting poet into school. Most writers are happy to tailor their input to suit children's needs – but discuss this in advance. If you want a hands-on creative writing session, check that your poet is happy to work with your chosen age-group.

● Poets are often booked months in advance, especially on occasions like National Poetry Day (October) or World Book Day (March). Plan well ahead.

● You will want as many children to benefit from your poet's visit as possible. However, if you spread the time too thinly, the benefits will be superficial. Perhaps every child can hear a reading, reserving workshops (if offered) for one or two groups to delve deeper into the writing process.

● Be sure to timetable follow-up work to get full advantage from the experience.

Tips, ideas and activities

● Prepare your children for their visitor. Do they know what a poet does; the poet's name? Show them how to look up the poet's name in the index of an anthology so that they know who to expect and what poems they have written.

● If you would you like your poet to stay after school and bring books along for signings and sale, let them know in advance. Decide whether to invite parents along after school. If your poet is travelling a long way, consider a two-day visit and perhaps schedule an INSET session if appropriate.

● If you plan to hot-seat your visitor, encourage the children to prepare pertinent questions. Spontaneity is good too, but sometimes children need time to prepare – especially if they are shy.

● Discuss ahead of the visit if your poet needs any special arrangements or props. Do they mind how the children are organised – seated at tables or with clipboards? Do they want questions saved for the end or are they happy to take them as they come? What size of group do they prefer?

● Be prepared to join in writing exercises yourself and experience first-hand how your children feel. At the same time, remember that poets are not teachers – even if some once were – and should not be left in charge of children. Classroom organisation and pupil control are up to you.

● Many publishers have links with writers and know who likes to work with which age-groups. Some may put you in contact with poets who visit schools. You could also surf the web as many poets have websites. Sometimes funding help is available from local arts associations.

● The following websites are worth a visit. Poetry Zone also publishes children's poetry on its site.
  ● www.poetrysociety.org.uk
  ● www.poetryzone.co.uk
  ● www.classactagency.co.uk

You Can... Create regular writing habits in children

Early years teachers have the privilege and responsibility of instilling good habits, benefiting child and teacher alike, for the whole of a child's school life. Top priority in writing must be 'name, date and title' on every piece of work – and name on the back of paintings. Chant it like a mantra until nobody forgets!

Thinking points

● Children can become unsettled by changes in routine, even if this is simply moving out of the normal classroom space. This is particularly so for those who have behavioural issues, because they need lots of structure.

● Some children (being children) will stretch the boundaries a bit when they move away from their desks and into a less confined space.

● Finding ways to encourage a calm atmosphere in the corridors and around the school is especially important in an open-plan school.

● Learning to have self-discipline outside the classroom will help the children to have consideration for others.

● Moving calmly through the corridors is important in maintaining a positive school ethos. It also helps to ensure that the children arrive at lessons in the appropriate frame of mind.

Tips, ideas and activities

● Ask children to keep daily diaries or weekly journals as a regular habit. Make this the first task on a Monday morning – if the children know that they are going to sit down and write on arrival, they can sort themselves out for the week's first few minutes. Make sure the new date is displayed.

● Handwriting practice is essential. Find ways to keep children's interest as they develop a style and begin to form letters that are consistent in size, direction and spacing. Poetry is useful as a text to copy as it contains a mixture of punctuation and includes capital letters. A poem using alliteration – or a tongue-twister – will provide ample practice of one particular letter. A Friday afternoon is perfect for the more technical side of writing.

● Encourage children to keep a reading diary, completing a page each time they finish reading a library book. (The writing frame on photocopiable page 57 will help.) For a change, suggest they write their own back-cover blurb instead.

● Following a session of creative play or art, encourage children to write their own annotations to their models or paintings. Model simple sentences such as: *I made this snail by rolling clay into a long string and curling it round and round.* Introduce writing in the third person about themselves – *John painted his cat chasing a butterfly.*

● For annotating children's models, keep a stock of cards, scored across the horizontal centre, ready to fold into a tent after writing. If children can see the purpose of annotation, and anticipate positioning their label beside their model, they will be more enthusiastic and careful while writing.

● At the end of the day, allow children to write their own reminders to take home: *Bring school trip money; Remember swimming kit.*

You Can... Integrate reading and writing skills

Reading and writing go hand in hand. As children begin to express themselves or demonstrate their knowledge in writing, they will increasingly turn to books for information and example. Copying text for handwriting practice is fine, but children need to learn how to be selective in what they copy, and to combine this with the ability to rephrase in their own words.

Thinking points

● Encourage children to précis orally what they hear you read to them. This serves as a forerunner to using information texts to aid their non-chronological writing.

● Ask questions about stories or texts that you have read to the class or that children have read for themselves, returning to the original source for confirmation.

● Demonstrate using an index and skimming text to look for key words to find out more about a subject.

● Encourage children to ask questions based on what you have read to them or they have read for themselves.

● Create word-banks, individually and as a class, to support children's writing. This may be topic-related or thematic in terms of the type of word – verbs, adjectives, joining words, days of the week, and so on.

Tips, ideas and activities

● Challenge children in groups to find out five facts about a chosen subject in five to ten minutes. Explain that they can use the index of non-fiction books to help. Allow them to draw on their own knowledge if appropriate. Explain that their five facts should be written in short, simple sentences.

● Listen to the five facts and encourage the children individually, or in pairs, to research each fact further and write two or three sentences about a selection of their facts, expanding each into a short paragraph or bullet point, depending on the style of writing required. For example, take the following fact on football: *A game requires two teams of eleven players.* This fact could be expanded to add a few sentences about players' positions and roles within the game; what kit they wear; at what distance the goals are positioned; the duration of a game and so on.

● As children delve deeper into their subjects they will inevitably require information that is not always in their heads. A selection of non-fiction texts, simple encyclopedias and thematic books will help them to find answers and support their writing.

● Choose subjects that offer a wide choice of interpretation, such as Wheels, as well as more closed subjects such as Foxes. Link your choice of subject matter with other curriculum areas, for example Things that float; Wet and dry; My home town and so on.

● Provide sticky markers to highlight text as the children read for information. They can draw an arrow on the end of a sticky-note to point at a key word or paragraph.

● Encourage children to create a short bibliography at the end of their non-fiction writing. This could be in as simple a form as: *These books helped me with my writing (title and author).*

You Can... Develop links between speaking and writing

For children to appreciate that writing is all about communication, they must first practise the skill of oral communication. Sharing news, retelling stories, asking and answering questions, commenting on the world around them, reading aloud – all such exchanges, one-to-one and in group and class conversation can serve to complement writing activities.

Thinking points

● Just as listening is to speaking, so reading is to writing. The two are mutually dependent. Reinforce the connection in children's minds by reading aloud what they have written and inviting comments and questions from their peers to encourage attentive listening.

● Teaching children how to listen to each other (encouraging eye contact and keeping still) will help speakers to gain confidence. This, in turn, will be reflected in the confidence of their subsequent written work.

● Inviting questions after explaining a written task will help diffident children to express any concerns. Be prepared to rephrase your requirements if children seem confused.

● Asking children to explain in their own words what you want them to do will confirm if they have understood what is required of them.

Tips, ideas and activities

● Most children enjoy telling their news – especially anything exciting: a wobbly tooth, a birthday party, a new pair of shoes. As children share news you can gradually encourage a level of formality that they won't experience at home or in the playground. This could include use of grammatically correct, formal English rather than the casual vernacular or colloquialisms. Reserve such corrections for more formal exchanges of thoughts, ideas and information.

● A fun way of encouraging infants to present to others in a more formal manner is to plan 'show and tell' sessions. Invite the children to prepare a short talk about something that interests them.

  ● As children plan for their show and tell, encourage them to write notes about what they are going to show. Ask the children to tell their partner a little about their choice and invite questions, noting questions and answers.

  ● Help the children to incorporate these notes into a series of numbered cards to act as cue cards when they give their presentation. Use photocopiable page 62 to help in the planning stage. Explain that they are not writing a script; a few key words to remind them what to say is sufficient. For example see the cards below.

  ● When children give their presentation, advise them to speak up, and ask listeners to save questions for the end. Encourage the speaker to stand at the front for greater audibility. Be prepared, if something being shown is fragile or valuable, to have a safe place to keep it during the remainder of the day.

Cue card 1:	Cue card 2:
• My hamster – its name, breed (if any) • Background – when, where, how got it • Age and expected lifespan	• Where it lives – how often it needs cleaning; how to go about it • Special needs – such as bedding materials

You Can... Initiate aids to effective writing

Early writers will have neither the expertise nor the motivation to turn to dictionaries to help them with their writing. They will draw on their phonic knowledge to work out spellings. To appreciate their efforts you must be ready to read children's independent, emerging writing with a similar approach in order to understand what they were aiming to write. Children are amazingly logical so follow the logic (aloud if necessary).

Thinking points

● If children are writing independent spellings such as 'mu-ay-d' for 'made' then the fault is with the teaching. Make sure you teach the simple phonic sound – in this case M saying *mmmm*; not *muh*.

● Display the alphabet chart plus digraphs, trigraphs and vowel combinations as and when they are taught so that they are visible for easy reference when children are writing.

● Keep charts of commonly used words, such as colour words and days of the week, as well as providing alphabetically arranged personal word-books for children to collect new words and spellings individually. Encourage them to include proper nouns such as elements of their home address, names of family members and pets, their school and teachers' names.

Tips, ideas and activities

● Encourage children to learn to write everyday words without looking. The 'look-say-cover-write-check' method works well.

● When children become stuck, try a variety of ways to practise their spelling: wooden or magnetic letters to rearrange; individual whiteboards and chalk boards to write and wipe; air-writing; tracing words or writing them with a finger in sand trays; forming the letters from Plasticine to arrange in order, until the tricky word is secure.

● Use mnemonics and rhymes to secure common spelling patterns, for example, long-vowel digraphs: *ea, ai, oa*:

When we go for walks, /It's the first one who talks, /And says their own name. *(See illustration: in this case 'a'.)*

● Make simple sentence-makers with generic opening words written on cards. Keep blanks for children to add words.

● Provide sets of flash-card topic words for each group. For example, the topic 'Me and My Family' might require flash cards such as: *house, flat, garden, pets*. Encourage children to copy these onto blanks and build up their sentence using their cards before writing it.

● Demonstrate how to use a simple spidergraph as a writing frame. Encourage children to develop each leg into a new sentence.

Where I live   Me   My family – mum, dad, sister
My age   What games I like to play

● The following sentences could emerge from the above: *I live in Spinney Street. I live with Mum, Dad and my sister, Nina. I am five-years-old. I like to play on my bike.*
● Expand, according to age and ability. An older, more confident writer might write a paragraph based on each spidergraph point and involving compound sentences.

You Can... **Help children improve accuracy**

Children beginning to gain confidence in writing will grow in enthusiasm. Re-reading their work to check for errors is not half as much fun as creating text in the first place. When time permits, reading it aloud to them, and highlighting word omissions or duplications, or adding punctuation, while explaining why, will model how they should approach the redrafting themselves.

Thinking points

● Model re-reading and redrafting newly created text during whole-class shared-writing so that children understand its purpose and how to set about the task.

● Offer children a simple checklist of areas to look at. You might use the mnemonic SWAP as a reminder: Spelling – especially high-frequency words; Words: missing/duplicated; Accuracy: checking if the end of a sentence matches its beginning, checking for sense; and Punctuation: full-stops/capital letters.

● Limit the areas for younger children to check according to your teaching focus. Sometimes, for example in emerging independent writing, you may decide not to worry unduly about spelling, but concentrate on simple sentence punctuation and application of capital letters.

● Determine how children can amend their writing with minimum mess to the original, for example use of an insertion mark while writing the missing word in the margin.

Tips, ideas and activities

● Children enjoy playing at 'being the teacher' marking work. Give them activity sheets of writing that contain errors. Tell them, for example, that there is one mistake in each line of text for them to discover.

● To retain freshness, occasionally allow the children to swap finished work with a partner and read each other's work, drawing attention to errors.

● Where children persistently make the same kind of error, make sure they understand what they are doing wrong. If an error recurs, check that you have explained the problem clearly.

● Encourage children, when proofreading their writing, to use their finger to point to their words as they read them, enabling them to check more carefully. Reading their work aloud also helps to reveal errors.

● Keep lists of high-frequency words handy for spellchecking and ask children to practise and learn words repeatedly misspelled as a separate activity.

● Where a rewrite of revised work is required, add an extra dimension so that the activity becomes a reward rather than a chore. Offer the children paper with a themed border to colour, or use plain paper with the option to illustrate their work. In the latter case, provide a sheet of ruled paper clipped behind the plain sheet as guidelines or use picture-and-story paper with dedicated drawing/writing areas (this can be created on a word processor with different shaped boxes for the children to write around).

You Can... **Develop effectiveness of writing**

The purpose of writing is as wide as human experience – from everyday personal lists and memos to letters, reports and books. Effective writing requires adopting the style of writing appropriate to its purpose. It is communicating with the reader – whether this is the writer themselves or a third party.

Thinking points

● Who and what am I writing this for? This is as valid a question for early years writing as for any other writing. It may be to practise scripting letters – getting *b*s and *d*s the right way round. It might be writing a story to entertain or a reminder for a very practical purpose. Matching style with purpose is the common factor.

● Explain the purpose of each writing activity so that children are aware of the area on which to focus their attention. Phrases such as *I shall be looking for…* and *I want to see…* clarify the aim.

● Where children display effective technique, share their work with the whole class by way of example and as inspiration to others to achieve equal success.

Tips, ideas and activities

● Check the register to see if any child's initials spell a word, such as Caroline Amy Russell. Demonstrate how writing *c-a-r* spells the word *car*. Show how writing this in capitals, C.A.R. reveals it to be initials. (The full stops tend to be ignored in modern usage. Their use can be described as 'optional' or, applying them to denote shortening, as 'traditional'.)

● Ask the children to write their full name, applying capitals to the first letter only of each name. Then ask them to write their initials. Invite them to practise writing their names with a title in front of their name – Miss, Ms or Mr – followed by initial(s) of forename(s) and full surname. Explain how this would appear on an envelope, formal invitation or form.

● Experiment with writing for different purposes, collecting useful phrases for greetings in letters and invitations.

● Create a cloze-procedure invitation for children to fill in details. This could be a genuine invitation, for example for parents to come to an open day. Alternatively, it could be a fictional invitation – inviting their favourite story-book character to a day in their class.

● Ask children to write a special personal message for Mother's Day cards saying 'thank you' for specific things mums do for them. Compare their informal and personal words with formal, impersonal greetings in commercial cards.

● Display the following as a short shopping list: *socks/lemonade/cakes/pen/notebook*. Alongside, display the following as a diary entry: *Monday: Went into town on 10am bus. Bought new blue socks to match my jumper. Got lemonade and cakes for my party. Planned invitations in my new notebook.* Discuss the different styles and how they serve different purposes.
  ● Ask the children to write a list of five items – either shopping or a to-do list – and turn these into a fictitious diary entry.

You Can... Encourage the use of word-processing

Seeing thoughts displayed as words on screen at the tap of a finger on the keyboard never ceases to fascinate children. With the addition of clip art or – better still – scanning in their own drawings for use in a word-processing program, children have a versatile writing tool literally at their fingertips. Using a traditional keyboard also helps to cement the connection between capital and lower-case letters.

Thinking points

● Ensure that seats allow children to sit at a computer comfortably and that they are able to use the keyboard and mouse with the screen positioned at eye level. Wherever possible, provide wrist support as the children use the mouse.

● If possible, provide an appropriate mouse position for left-handed members of your class.

● Use an interactive whiteboard to demonstrate word-processing software so that all children can see easily. Demonstrate how to insert clip art or children's own previously scanned drawings or digital photos.

● Show children how easily errors are rectified electronically, compared with corrections to handwritten work.

● Limit word-processing work to short sessions, as children may be slow at first at finding their way around the keyboard.

Tips, ideas and activities

● Scan in children's pictures and invite them to type a caption. Similarly, photographs taken of the children in class make a good starting prompt for writing about themselves. Such images also offer possibilities for varying the presentation of text. For example, words might be made to appear in a speech bubble linked to the child's photograph or drawing.

● Provide unpunctuated text for children to practise selecting and changing appropriate letters to capitals and adding punctuation. Similarly, create cloze procedures where children can type into the spaces.

● Key in children's handwritten work and encourage them to improve and change their text on screen. They can experiment with font and appearance (underlining, bold, italic). Show how titles can be centred.

● Suggest that older children could begin to use a thesaurus, integral to the word-processing program, selecting more effective adjectives or verbs for example. Discuss how playing with text size can have graphic impact, such as making the word *big* bigger than others or the word *small*, smaller.

● Model how to use a spellchecker and how to add words to a personal electronic dictionary, such as the child's own name.

● Demonstrate how to use shortcut keys to move the cursor to the beginning or end of a line.

● Help older or more confident children to learn how to cut and paste single words or sections of text to change the word order. Practise this by keying in sentences where one word is out of place for them to spot and correct.

● When children are able to key in copies of their hand-drafted work, help them to insert scanned images and drawings to enhance the finished work.

You Can... **Link writing to other areas of the curriculum**

Aspects of writing inevitably enter other areas of the curriculum by default: note-taking from oral and visual resources, recording observations, labelling diagrams and simple bar charts, and so on. Even in an early years classroom, there are many opportunities for children's writing to cross curriculum boundaries.

Thinking points

● When planning activities, look for opportunities to combine objectives. Writing labels and captions, for example, is easily and naturally imbedded within almost any topic work.

● When preparing text for an activity sheet for the children to embellish, select subject matter that is relevant to current topic work. If the object of the exercise is to reorder a jumbled sentence, there is no reason why that sentence should not reflect another area of study: *autumn some lose trees their In leaves!*

● Children still practising writing their names will enjoy writing them in special shapes or on coloured paper, linking to art. A bar-chart of 'How I come to school' or 'My birthday month', links writing skills with maths and geography or science.

Tips, ideas and activities

● How many times can a child throw a ball and catch it – or bounce it – before they drop the ball? Their partner can count. They can then write simple sentences about their findings: *Jack bounced the ball three times. Chloe bounced the ball once.* Now ask them to write a comparative statement: *Jack bounced the ball two more times than Chloe. Jack bounced the ball longer than Chloe.* Already, PE, maths and English are all combined. An alternative, involving measurement skills, would be *How far can you roll a ball?*

● Next, introduce science to the activity. Create a collection of different balls and compare their materials, their construction, their ability to bounce, float, and so on. Suggest that the children record their findings in various forms, such as lists under headings, or simple sentences – *tennis balls are made of two tessellating pieces stuck together. They are rubber covered in felt. Tennis balls are hollow and yellow. They bounce. Rugby balls are not round.* So, here we have maths: sorting, and science: materials – more areas of the curriculum linked with simple sentence-writing.

● Invite children to invent their own ball game and write a simple set of rules.

● Tell the story of the little boy who would not share. He had a cricket set but when others showed an interest in his new toys he clutched them to him and would not let them touch. 'My bat. My ball. My wickets!' he cried. So he never got to play a single game of cricket because he never learned to share and you can't play cricket on your own. Invite the children to discuss the story – combining speaking and listening skills with PSHE.

● Invite the children to discuss, devise and write down a list of rules for sharing in school.

You Can... **Demonstrate practical uses of writing**

Consider for a minute the amount and variety of pieces of printed paper that will cross your path today: newspapers, letters, junk mail, advertising flyers, business reports, bank statements, work records and plans, notices, reminders, memos, lists, notes from parents, notes to go home, marks sheets, registers, and so it goes on. Where would we be without writing?

Thinking points

● Hold up a few examples of written communications that you are dealing with today and explain to the children that people have sat down and written all these things, each with a different purpose. Point out how this demonstrates the importance of writing.

● Letter writing is one of the first forms of purposeful writing that a child will encounter outside school. As a literacy task it is useful for teaching many aspects of writing, from the use of capitals at the beginning of proper nouns and sentences, to the exclusive idiosyncrasy of a personal signature, as distinct from printing your name.

● Preserving anonymity, share or paraphrase some excuse, permission or explanatory note from parents. Explain how these differ from word-of-mouth messages. They include a date, an address and a signature. Details can be re-read, avoiding ambiguity. Compare the permanence of letters with the transitory nature of speech.

Tips, ideas and activities

● Explain that the purpose of all writing is communication, but that letter-writing is very specific in this. A letter is often to one person from one other person, in order to relay important information or news; it is a way of 'speaking' in a way that can be read and re-read – like replaying a tape.

● Demonstrate the basic layout of a letter including address, date, Dear and a closing phrase such as *Love from*, *Yours sincerely* or *Best wishes*.

  ● Invite children to write their own letter, putting in personal details. They might imagine they are writing a thank-you letter to an aunt or uncle. Let them choose what present or kind help they have received or suggest that the relative has sent them money. Ask them to write why the choice of present was a good one and/or how they spent the money or benefited from the kindness.

● For younger children, a less formal but useful exercise is writing a postcard. This still involves writing an address – they can 'send' a postcard home with their own address and discover how Mum and Dad have formal names and titles, too. Give children a blank postcard. Ask them to draw and colour a picture on the plain side. On the other, show how one side is reserved for a message, the other for an address and the recipient's name. Their message need only be brief.

  ● Involve the children's imaginations – a postcard from the moon; a postcard from their pet rabbit writing from the bottom of the garden; a postcard from Father Christmas. If funds permit, allow the children to post these home to reinforce the experience of writing something to be read later. Make sure that you use a standard post-office sized card.

You Can... **Incorporate experiences into writing**

Teachers are often terrible hoarders – they can't throw anything away. Now is your chance to justify all that hoarding (and clutter-clear at the same time!). Collect a pile of periodicals, holiday brochures, TV magazines and postcards. Cut out and mount pictures and sort them into people and places. Laminate them, to lengthen their durability, and you will have created an invaluable classroom resource.

Thinking points

● Pictures of local places or generically familiar places (supermarkets, parks, zoos and so on) are great conversation pieces for young children who can identify with scenes through personal experience.

● All language activity, commenting and describing, assessing and discussing, results from and provokes thought. Thoughts become spoken words and spoken words become written words. Non-fiction writing is not simply factual, it can express opinion.

● For children not yet ready to write sentences, the use of speech marks and thought bubbles, superimposed upon pictures, allows simple practice at writing sounds and words.

Tips, ideas and activities

● Using a word-processing program, insert, enlarge and print some speech bubbles, thought bubbles and exclamation 'call-outs'. Alternatively draw and photocopy some of your own.

● Print some of these on laminated sheets to be transparent and reusable with wipeable fibre-tip ink pens.

● Give out pictures for children to look at and discuss what is happening. Who is thinking and saying what?

● Depending on the area of writing you want the children to practise, advise them what to write in the 'call-out' shapes. For example, you might tell the children that you want someone in the picture to be saying *no* or *yes* or *look*; another might be saying *gr* or *mmm* as though they are cross about something or are anticipating an icecream! Invite the children, having written in their call-out shapes, to glue them in position on their picture.

● Create a wall-frieze of the school playground or a school outing. Ask each child to paint their own figure portrait to go into the large-scale picture. Each can then add a scaled-up 'call-out' message to the scene. Challenge them to think up a word or sound that no-one else has used. Or, invite children to work in pairs, choosing the same sound or word. Stick these on in different positions and challenge the children to find pairs of matching words. (If you pin rather than stick the callout shapes in place, they can be rearranged to vary the matching game.)

Mixed-up sentences

- The words in these sentences are mixed up.
- Sort them and write them on the lines.
- Each sentence starts with a capital letter.

fell Jack down.

_____

tumbling Jill after came.

_____

clock the mouse up ran The.

_____

to began birds The sing.

_____

a stepped puddle in He.

_____

tree little nut had I a.

_____

met Simple a Simon pieman.

_____

in Little Jack corner sat Horner the.

_____

out sea Swan to swam.

_____

My book review

Title _____

Author _____

The main character in this story was _____

The story was about _____

_____

_____

_____

The part I liked best was _____

_____

_____

Here is a quotation copied from the story

_____

_____

_____

I chose this because it shows

_____

_____

Good news, bad news

Main character:

Opening setting and character's opening activity:

Good news: Bad news:

Ending:

Story dice

- Throw dice to decide on elements of your fantasy story.

Main character

1. Snowman   **3.** Alien from another planet   **5.** Mermaid
2. Elf   **4.** Teddy bear   **6.** Rabbit

Other main characters

- Shake twice: choose one as a trickster and one as a helper to your main character:

1. Talking bird or fish   **3.** Wizard   **5.** Flying banana
2. Fairy   **4.** Matchstick man   **6.** Talking flower

- Remember you can add other characters to your story if you need them.

Setting

1. Fairground or circus   **3.** Seaside or undersea   **5.** School playground
2. Forest   **4.** Shopping arcade   **6.** Mountains or inside a mountain

Main Character's problem (central to the plot):

1. Lost – themselves, someone or something else
2. Lonely – wants to make friends
3. Wants to escape from someone or somewhere
4. Hurt or injured – needs help
5. Wants to go somewhere or see someone special
6. Bored and wants adventure and excitement

Plot plan – how your main character's problem is solved.
Remember: they will get help, but first they get tricked!

Poems with simple structures

MAGPIE RHYME

One for sorrow,
Two for joy,
Three for a girl,
Four for a boy.

Five for silver,
Six for gold,
Seven for a secret
Never to be told.

Traditional

DAFFODIL DIP

Dip, dip, daffodil, trumpet shout.
Dip, dip, daffodil, you are OUT.

Celia Warren

WHEN THE WIND IS IN THE EAST

When the wind is in the East
'Tis neither good for man nor beast.

When the wind is in the North
The skilful fisher goes not forth.

When the wind is in the South
It blows the bait in the fish's mouth.

When the wind is in the West,
Then it's at its very best.

Traditional

THE SWING

How do you like to go up in a swing,
Up in the air so blue?
Oh, I do think it is the pleasantest thing
Ever a child can do!

Up in the air and over the wall,
Till I can see so wide,
Rivers and trees and cattle and all
Over the countryside.

Till I look down on the garden green,
Down on the roof so brown –
Up in the air I go flying again,
Up in the air and down!

Robert Louis Stevenson

WHO AM I?

Dainty wings so fine and bright,
That flutter in my silent flight.
When I was young I had no wings at all
Who am I who used to crawl?

Slowly, slowly, house upon my back,
I creep along and leave a silver track.
Inside my shell I hide from every thrush
Who am I who's never in a rush?

Celia Warren

Find the rhymes

I can find rhymes...

• Ring the words that rhyme with the word in the box.

cat   fat   mat   net   hop   hat   lap   rat   chat

say   day   sky   hay   away   eye   you   lay   may

I can make up rhymes...

shop   ....

will   ....

I can use alliteration...

Pretty, pink pompoms.

A .... morning.

......................, ... balloons.

.... shoes.

The ...., ... frog.

......................, ... lanes.

......................, ..., ...

funny   long   frisky   lovely   blue   shiny   bright   misty

I can use repetition...

Bang, bang, bang, said the drum!

......................, ..., ... said the sea!

......................, ..., ... said the wind.

Show and tell

I plan to show and tell everyone about my

_____

_____

Introduction and background information

Basic details – facts and figures

| 2 |

More information in greater detail

Summing up (such as, why you recommended this)

Index

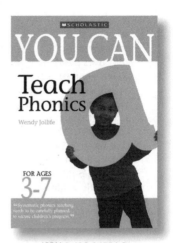

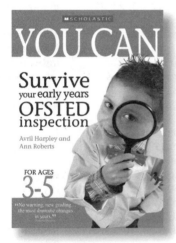

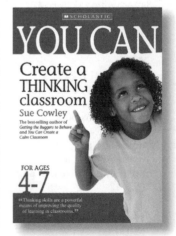